New Perspectives on

MICROSOFT®
WORD® 2000

Brief

S. SCOTT ZIMMERMAN
Brigham Young University

BEVERLY B. ZIMMERMAN
Brigham Young University

ANN SHAFFER

COURSE
TECHNOLOGY

Thomson Learning™

ONE MAIN STREET, CAMBRIDGE, MA 02142

Australia • Canada • Denmark • Japan • Mexico • New Zealand • Philippines
Puerto Rico • Singapore • South Africa • Spain • United Kingdom • United States

New Perspectives on Microsoft® Word® 2000—Brief is published by Course Technology.

Senior Editor	Donna Gridley	Developmental Editor	Robin Romer
Senior Product Manager	Rachel Crapser	Production Editor	Daphne Barbas
Product Manager	Catherine Donaldson	Text Designer	Meral Dabcovich
Associate Product Manager	Karen Shortill	Cover Art Designer	Douglas Goodman
Editorial Assistant	Melissa Dezotell		

© 1999 by Course Technology, a division of Thomson Learning

For more information contact:

Course Technology
One Main Street
Cambridge, MA 02142
Or find us on the World Wide Web at: http://www.course.com

Asia (excluding Japan):
Thomson Learning
60 Albert Street, #15-01
Albert Complex
Singapore 189969

Latin America:
Thomson Learning
Seneca, 53
Colonia Polanco
11560 Mexico D.F. Mexico

Japan:
Thomson Learning
Palaceside Building 5F
1-1-1 Hitotsubashi, Chiyoda-ku
Tokyo 100 0003 Japan

South Africa:
Thomson Learning
Zonnebloem Building,
Constantia Square
526 Sixteenth Road
P.O. Box 2459
Halfway House, 1685
South Africa

Canada:
Nelson/Thomson Learning
1120 Birchmount Road
Scarborough, Ontario
Canada M1K 5G4

UK/Europe/Middle East:
Thomson Learning
Berkshire House
168-173 High Holborn
London
WC1V 7AA United Kingdom

Business Press/Thomson Learning
Berkshire House
168-173 High Holborn
London WC1V 7AA United Kingdom

Thomson Nelson & Sons LTD
Nelson House
Mayfield Road
Walton-on-Thames
KT12 5PL United Kingdom

Australia/New Zealand:
Nelson/Thomson Learning
102 Dodds Street
South Melbourne, Victoria 3205

Spain
Paraninfo/Thomson Learning
Calle Magallanes, 25
28015-MADRID
ESPANA

Distrubution Services:
Thomson Learning
Ceriton House
North Way
Andover, Hampshire SP10 5BE

International Headquarters:
Thomson Learning
International Division
290 Harbor Drive, 2nd Floor
Stamford, CT 06902-7477

Trademarks

Course Technology and the Open Book logo are registered trademarks and CourseKits is a trademark of Course Technology. Custom Edition is a registered trademark of Thomson Learning.

The Thomson Learning Logo is a registered trademark used herein under license.

Some of the product names and company names used in this book have been used for identification purposes only and may be trademarks or registered trademarks of their respective manufacturers and sellers.

Microsoft and the Office logo are either registered trademarks or trademarks of Microsoft Corporation in the United States and/or other countries. Course Technology is an independent entity from Microsoft Corporation, and not affiliated with Microsoft in any manner.

Disclaimer

Course Technology reserves the right to revise this publication and make changes from time to time in its content without notice.

ISBN 0-7600-6991-3

Printed in the United States of America

6 7 8 9 10 BM 04 03 02 01

PREFACE

The New Perspectives Series

About New Perspectives

Course Technology's **New Perspectives Series** is an integrated system of instruction that combines text and technology products to teach computer concepts, the Internet, and microcomputer applications. Users consistently praise this series for innovative pedagogy, use of interactive technology, creativity, accuracy, and supportive and engaging style.

How is the New Perspectives Series different from other series?

The **New Perspectives Series** distinguishes itself by **innovative technology**, from the renowned Course Labs to the state-of-the-art multimedia that is integrated with our Concepts texts. Other distinguishing features include **sound instructional design, proven pedagogy,** and **consistent quality.** Each tutorial has students learn features in the context of solving a realistic case problem rather than simply learning a laundry list of features. With the **New Perspectives Series,** instructors report that students have a complete, integrative learning experience that stays with them. They credit this high retention and competency to the fact that this series incorporates critical thinking and problem-solving with computer skills mastery. In addition, we work hard to ensure accuracy by using a multi-step quality assurance process during all stages of development. Instructors focus on teaching and students spend more time learning.

What course is this book appropriate for?

New Perspectives on Microsoft® Word® 2000— Brief can be used in any course in which you want students to learn the essential topics of Microsoft Word 2000, including planning, creating, and editing a document, creating a multiple-page report, and desktop publishing a document. It is particularly recommended for a short course on Word. This book assumes that students have learned basic Windows 95, 98, or NT navigation and file management skills from Course Technology's *New Perspectives on Microsoft Windows 95—Brief,* or the equivalent book for Windows 98 or NT.

Proven Pedagogy

Tutorial **Tips** ⊢

Tutorial Tips Page This page, following the Table of Contents, offers students suggestions on how to effectively plan their study and lab time, what to do when they make a mistake, how to use the Reference Windows, MOUS grids, Quick Checks, and other features of the New Perspectives Series.

CASE

Tutorial Case Each tutorial begins with a problem presented in a case that is meaningful to students. The case turns the task of learning how to use an application into a problem-solving process.

45-minute Sessions Each tutorial is divided into sessions that can be completed in about 45 minutes to an hour. Sessions allow instructors to more accurately allocate time in their syllabus, and students to better manage their own study time.

1.

2.

3.

Step-by-Step Methodology We make sure students can differentiate between what they are to *do* and what they are to *read*. Through numbered steps—clearly identified by a gray shaded background—students are constantly guided in solving the case problem. In addition, the numerous screen shots with callouts direct students' attention to what they should look at on the screen.

TROUBLE?

TROUBLE? Paragraphs These paragraphs anticipate the mistakes or problems that students may have and help them continue with the tutorial.

Read

"Read This Before You Begin" Page Located opposite the first tutorial's opening page for each section of the text, the Read This Before You Begin Page helps introduce technology into the classroom. Technical considerations and assumptions about software are listed to save

QUICK CHECK

RW

TASK REFERENCE

REVIEW

CASE

INTERNET

LAB

time and eliminate unnecessary aggravation. Notes about the Data Disks help instructors and students get their files in the right places, so students get started on the right foot.

Quick Check Questions Each session concludes with meaningful, conceptual Quick Check questions that test students' understanding of what they learned in the session. Answers to the Quick Check questions are provided at the end of each tutorial.

Reference Windows Reference Windows are succinct summaries of the most important tasks covered in a tutorial and they preview actions students will perform in the steps to follow.

Task Reference Located as a table at the end of the book, the Task Reference contains a summary of how to perform common tasks using the most efficient method, as well as references to pages where the task is discussed in more detail.

End-of-Tutorial Review Assignments, Case Problems, Internet Assignments, and Lab Assignments Tutorial Assignments provide students with additional hands-on practice of the skills they learned in the tutorial using the same case presented in the tutorial. These Assignments are followed by three to four Case Problems that have approximately the same scope as the tutorial case but use a different scenario. In addition, some of the Tutorial Assignments or Case Problems may include Exploration Exercises that challenge students, encourage them to explore the capabilities of the program they are using, and/or further extend their knowledge. Each tutorial also includes instructions on getting to the text's Student Online Companion page, which contains the Internet Assignments and other related links for the text. Internet Assignments are additional exercises that integrate the skills the students learned in the tutorial with the World Wide Web. Finally, if a Course Lab accompanies a tutorial, Lab Assignments are included after the Case Problems.

New Perspectives on Microsoft® Word® 2000—Brief Instructor's Resource Kit for this title contains:

- ■ Electronic Instructor's Manual
- ■ Data Files
- ■ Solution Files
- ■ Course Test Manager Testbank
- ■ Course Test Manager Engine
- ■ Figure Files

These supplements come on CD-ROM. If you don't have access to a CD-ROM drive, contact your Course Technology customer service representative for more information.

Acknowledgments

Sincere thanks to the reviewers for their excellent feedback: Calleen Coorough, Skagit Valley College; Bonnie Bailey, Moorhead State; Janet Sheppard, Collin County Community College; Ralph Brasure, Liberty University; Mary Dobranski, College of St. Mary; and Tony Gabriel, Computer Learning Center. Thanks also go out to John Bosco, Quality Assurance Project Leader, and Nicole Ashton, John Freitas, Alex White, and Jeff Schwartz, QA testers, for verifying the technical accuracy of every step.

Many thanks to all the smart, friendly, helpful folks at Course Technology, including Melissa Dezotell, for managing the review process so smoothly; Karen Shortill, for her expertise on the supplements; and Catherine Donaldson, for all her contributions. In particular, thanks to Rachel Crapser, product manager, for steering us through the rough waters of the Office 2000 beta with so much professionalism and good cheer. Thanks to Robin Romer, development editor, for her encouraging phone calls and expert editing. Thank you to Daphne Barbas, production editor, for magically transforming the manuscript into a published book.

Ann Shaffer, S. Scott Zimmerman, & Beverly Zimmerman

I also owe a great debt to Beverly and Scott Zimmerman, writers and teachers extraordinaire, for giving me the opportunity to be a part of their team. And special thanks to Lois Sachtjen, for being such a kind and helpful friend.

Ann Shaffer

TABLE OF CONTENTS

Reference **Window List**

Tutorial **Tips**

These tutorials will help you learn about Microsoft Word 2000. The tutorials are designed to be worked through at a computer. Each tutorial is divided into sessions. Watch for the session headings, such as Session 1.1 and Session 1.2. Each session is designed to be completed in about 45 minutes, but take as much time as you need. It's also a good idea to take a break between sessions.

Before you begin, read the following questions and answers. They will help you plan your time and use the tutorials effectively.

Where do I start?

Each tutorial begins with a case, which sets the scene for the tutorial and gives you background information to help you understand what you will be doing. Read the case before you go to the lab. In the lab, begin with the first session of a tutorial.

How do I know what to do on the computer?

Each session contains steps that you will perform on the computer to learn how to use Microsoft Word 2000. Read the text that introduces each series of steps. The steps you need to do at a computer are numbered and are set against a shaded background. Read each step carefully and completely before you try it.

How do I know if I did the step correctly?

As you work, compare your computer screen with the corresponding figure in the tutorial. Don't worry if your screen display is somewhat different from the figure. The important parts of the screen display are labeled in each figure. Check to make sure these parts are on your screen.

What if I make a mistake?

Don't worry about making mistakes—they are part of the learning process. Paragraphs labeled "TROUBLE?" identify common problems and explain how to get back on track. Follow the steps in a TROUBLE? paragraph only if you are having the problem described. If you run into other problems:

- Carefully consider the current state of your system, the position of the pointer, and any messages on the screen.

- Complete the sentence, "Now I want to…" Be specific, because identifying your goal will help you rethink the steps you need to take to reach that goal.

- If you are working on a particular piece of software, consult the Help system.

- If the suggestions above don't solve your problem, consult your technical support person for assistance.

How do I use the Reference Windows?

Reference Windows summarize the procedures you will learn in the tutorial steps. Do not complete the actions in the Reference Windows when you are working through the tutorial. Instead, refer to the Reference Windows while you are working on the assignments at the end of the tutorial.

How can I test my understanding of the material I learned in the tutorial?

At the end of each session, you can answer the list of Quick Check questions. The answers for the Quick Checks are at the end of that tutorial.

After you have completed the entire tutorial, you should complete the Review Assignments and Case Problems. They are carefully structured so that you will review what you have learned and then apply your knowledge to new situations.

What if I can't remember how to do something?

You should refer to the Task Reference at the end of the book; it summarizes how to accomplish tasks using the most efficient method.

Before you begin the tutorials, you should know the basics about your computer's operating system. You should also know how to use the menus, dialog boxes, Help system, and My Computer.

Now that you've read the Tutorial Tips, you are ready to begin.

New Perspectives on

MICROSOFT® WORD® 2000

Read This Before You Begin

To the Student

Data Disks

To complete the Level I tutorials, Review Assignments, and Case Problems, you need 1 Data Disk. Your instructor will either provide you with this Data Disk or ask you to make your own.

If you are making your own Data Disk, you will need 1 blank, formatted high-density disk. You will need to copy a set of folders from a file server or standalone computer or the Web onto your disks. Your instructor will tell you which computer, drive letter, and folders contain the files you need. You could also download the files by going to www.course.com, clicking Data Disk Files, and following the instructions on the screen.

The following shows you which folders go on your disk, so that you will have enough disk space to complete all the tutorials, Review Assignments, and Case Problems:

Data Disk 1

Write this on the disk label:
Data Disk 1: Word 2000 Tutorials 1-4

Put these folders on the disk:
Tutorial.01, Tutorial.02, Tutorial.03, Tutorial.04

When you begin each tutorial, be sure you are using the correct Data Disk. Refer to the "File Finder" Chart at the back of this text for more detailed information on which files are used in which tutorials. See the inside front cover of this book for more information on Student Disk files, or ask your instructor or technical support person for assistance.

Course Labs

The Word Level I tutorials feature an interactive Course Lab to help you understand word processing concepts. There are Lab Assignments at the end of Tutorial 1 that relate to this Lab.

To start a Lab, click the **Start** button on the Windows taskbar, point to **Programs**, point to **Course Labs**, point to **New Perspectives Course Labs**, and click the name of the Lab you want to use.

Using Your Own Computer

If you are going to work through this book using your own computer, you need:

- **Computer System** Microsoft Windows 95, 98, NT, or higher must be installed on your computer. This book assumes a typical installation of Microsoft Word.

- **Data Disk** You will not be able to complete the tutorials or exercises in this book using your own computer until you have your Data Disk.

- **Course Labs** See your instructor or technical support person to obtain the Course Lab software for use on your own computer.

Visit Our World Wide Web Site

Additional materials designed especially for you are available on the World Wide Web. Go to http://www.course.com.

To the Instructor

The Data Files and Course Labs are available on the Instructor's Resource Kit for this title. Follow the instructions in the Help file on the CD-ROM to install the programs to your network or standalone computer. For information on creating Data Disks or the Course Labs, see the "To the Student" section above.

In this tutorial you will:

- Start and exit Word

- Identify the components of the Word window

- Choose commands using the toolbars and menus

- Create and edit a document

- Enter the date with AutoComplete

- Correct spelling errors with AutoCorrect

- Scroll through a document

- Save, preview, and print a document

- Record properties for a document

- Use the Word Help system to get help

LAB

Word Processing

CREATING A DOCUMENT

Writing a Business Letter for Crossroads

CASE

Crossroads

Karen Liu is executive director of Crossroads, a small, nonprofit organization in Tacoma, Washington. Crossroads distributes business clothing to low-income clients who are returning to the job market or starting new careers. To make potential clients in the community more aware of their services, Crossroads reserves an exhibit booth each year at a local job fair sponsored by the Tacoma Chamber of Commerce. Crossroads needs to find out the date and location of this year's fair, as well as some other logistical information, before reserving a booth. Karen asks you to write a letter requesting this information from the Tacoma Chamber of Commerce.

In this tutorial you will create Karen's letter using Microsoft Word 2000, a popular word-processing program. Before you begin typing the letter, you will learn to start the Word program, identify and use the elements of the Word screen, and adjust some Word settings. Next you will create a new Word document, type the text of the Crossroads letter, save the letter, and then print the letter for Karen. In the process of entering the text, you'll learn several ways of correcting typing errors. You'll also find out how to use the Word Help system, which allows you to quickly find answers to your questions about the program.

Four Steps to a Professional Document

Word helps you produce quality work in minimal time. Not only can you type a document in Word, you can quickly make revisions and corrections, adjust margins and spacing, create columns and tables, and add graphics to your documents. The most efficient way to produce a document is to follow these four steps: (1) planning and creating, (2) editing, (3) formatting, and (4) printing.

In the long run, *planning* saves time and effort. First, you should determine what you want to say. State your purpose clearly and include enough information to achieve that purpose without overwhelming or boring your reader. Be sure to *organize* your ideas logically. Also, decide how you want your document to look. In this case, your letter to the Tacoma Chamber of Commerce will take the form of a standard business letter. Karen has given you a handwritten note with all her questions for the Tacoma Chamber of Commerce, as shown in Figure 1-1.

Figure 1-1	KAREN'S QUESTIONS ABOUT THE JOB FAIR

Please write the Tacoma Chamber of Commerce and find out the following:

What are the location and dates for this year's job fair?

Is a map of the exhibit area available? What size booths are available and how can we reserve a booth?

Who do we contact about what physical facilities are available at each booth?

Send the letter to the Chamber's president. The address is 210 Shoreline Vista, Suite 1103, Tacoma WA 98402.

After you've planned your document, you can go ahead and *create* it using Word. The next step, *editing*, consists of reading the document you've created, then correcting your errors, and, finally, adding or deleting text to make the document easy to read.

Once your document is error-free, you can *format* it to make it visually appealing. Formatting features, such as white space (blank areas of a page), line spacing, boldface, and italics can help make your document easier to read. *Printing* is the final phase in creating an effective document. In this tutorial, you will preview your document before you spend time and resources to print it.

Starting Word

Before you can apply these four steps to produce a letter in Word, you need to start Word and learn about the general organization of the Word screen. You'll do that now.

To start Microsoft Word:

1. Make sure Windows is running on your computer and the Windows desktop appears on your screen.

2. Click the **Start** button on the taskbar to display the Start menu, and then point to **Programs** to display the Programs menu.

3. Point to **Microsoft Word** on the Programs menu. See Figure 1-2.

| Figure 1-2 | STARTING MICROSOFT WORD |

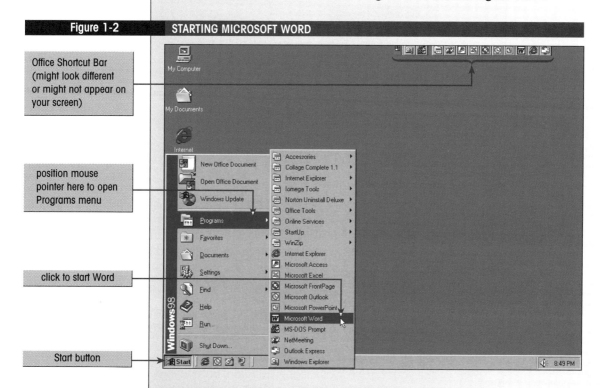

Office Shortcut Bar (might look different or might not appear on your screen)

position mouse pointer here to open Programs menu

click to start Word

Start button

TROUBLE? Don't worry if your screen differs slightly from Figure 1-2. Although the figures in this book were created while running Windows 98 in its default settings, these operating systems share the same basic user interface. Microsoft Word should run equally well using Windows 95, Windows 98 in Web style, Windows NT, or Windows 2000.

TROUBLE? If you don't see the Microsoft Word option on the Programs menu, ask your instructor or technical support person for help.

TROUBLE? If the Office Shortcut Bar appears on your screen, your system is set up to display it. Because the Office Shortcut Bar is not required to complete these tutorials, it has been omitted from the remaining figures in this text. You can close it or simply ignore it.

4. Click **Microsoft Word**. After a short pause, the Microsoft Word copyright information appears in a message box and remains on the screen until the Word program window, containing a blank Word document, is displayed. See Figure 1-3.

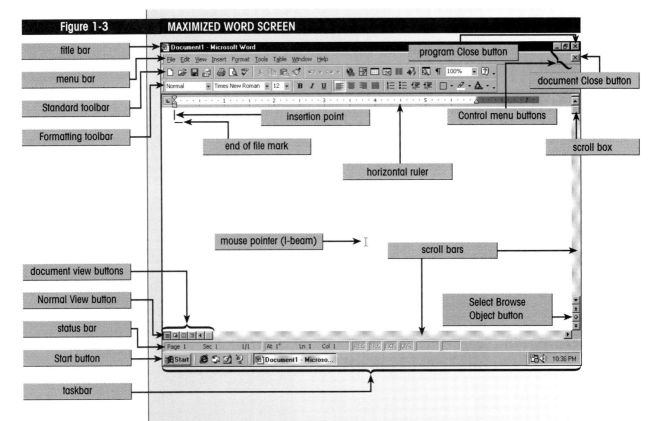

Figure 1-3   MAXIMIZED WORD SCREEN

TROUBLE? Depending on how your system is set up, the Office Assistant might open when you start Word. For now, click Help on the menu bar, and then click Hide the Office Assistant. You'll learn more about the Office Assistant later in this tutorial. If you've just installed Microsoft Word, you'll need to click the Start Using Microsoft Word button, which the Office Assistant displays, before closing the Office Assistant window.

5. If the Word window does not fill the entire screen, click the **Maximize** button in the upper-right corner of the Word window. Your screen should now resemble Figure 1-3.

TROUBLE? If your screen looks slightly different from Figure 1-3 (for example, if you see the paragraph mark character ¶ on your screen, the Standard and Formatting toolbars appear on one row, or an additional toolbar is displayed), just continue with the steps. You will learn how to make some adjustments to the Word screen shortly.

Word is now running and ready to use.

Viewing the Word Screen

The Word screen is made up of a number of elements, each of which is described in Figure 1-4. You are already familiar with some of these elements, such as the menu bar, title bar, and status bar, because they are common to all Windows screens.

If at any time you would like to check the name of a Word toolbar button, just position the mouse pointer over the button without clicking. A **ScreenTip**, a small yellow box with the name of the button, will appear.

Figure 1-4	DESCRIPTION OF WORD SCREEN ELEMENTS
SCREEN ELEMENT	**DESCRIPTION**
Control menu buttons	Size and close the Word window and the document
Document Close button	Closes the open document when only one document is open
Document view buttons	Switch the document between four different views: normal view, Web layout view, print layout view, and outline view
Document window	Area where you enter text and graphics
End-of-file mark	Indicates the end of the document
Formatting toolbar	Contains buttons to activate common font and paragraph formatting commands
Horizontal ruler	Adjusts margins, tabs, and column widths; vertical ruler appears in print layout view
Insertion point	Indicates location where characters will be inserted or deleted
Menu bar	Contains lists or menus of all the Word commands. When you first display a menu, you see a short list of the most frequently used commands. To see the full list of commands in the menu, you can either click the menu and then wait a few seconds for the remaining commands to appear or click the menu and then click or point to the downward-facing double-arrow at the bottom of the menu.
Mouse pointer	Changes shape depending on its location on the screen (i.e., I-beam pointer in text area; arrow in nontext areas)
Program Close button	Closes the current document if more than one document is open. Closes Word if one or no document is open.
Scroll bars	Shifts text vertically and horizontally on the screen so you can see different parts of the document
Scroll box	Helps you move quickly to other pages of your document
Select Browse Object button	Displays buttons that allow you to move quickly through the document
Standard toolbar	Contains buttons to activate frequently used commands
Start button	Starts a program, opens a document, provides quick access to Windows Help
Status bar	Provides information regarding the location of the insertion point
Taskbar	Shows programs that are running and allows you to switch quickly from one program to another
Title bar	Identifies the current application (i.e., Microsoft Word); shows the filename of the current document

Keep in mind that the commands on the menu bars initially display the commands that are used most frequently on your particular computer. When you leave the menu displayed for a few seconds or point to the double-arrow, a more complete list of commands appears. Throughout these tutorials, point to the double-arrow if you do not see the command you need.

Checking the Screen Before You Begin Each Tutorial

Word provides a set of standard settings, called **default settings**, that are appropriate for most documents. However, the setup of your Word document might have different default settings from those shown in the figures. This often happens when you share a computer and another user changes the appearance of the Word screen. The rest of this section explains what your screen should look like and how to make it match those in the tutorials.

Setting the Document View to Normal

You can view your document in one of four ways—normal, Web layout, print layout, or outline. **Web layout view** and **outline view** are designed for special situations that you don't need to worry about now. You will, however, learn more about **print layout view**—which allows you to see a page's design and format—in later tutorials. You will use **normal view**, which allows you to see more of the document, for this tutorial. Depending on the document view selected by the last person who used Word, you might need to change the document back to normal view.

To make sure the document window is in normal view:

1. Click the **Normal View** button ▤ to the left of the horizontal scroll bar. See Figure 1-5. If your document window was not in normal view, it changes to normal view now. The Normal View button looks pressed in to indicate that it is selected.

Figure 1-5	CHANGING TO NORMAL VIEW

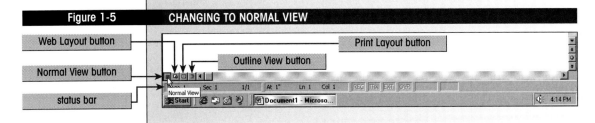

Web Layout button

Print Layout button

Outline View button

Normal View button

status bar

Displaying the Toolbars and Ruler

These tutorials frequently use the Standard toolbar and the Formatting toolbar to help you work more efficiently. Each time you start Word, check to make sure both toolbars appear on your screen, with the Standard toolbar on top of the Formatting toolbar. Depending on the settings specified by the last person to use your computer, you may not see both toolbars, or your toolbars may appear all on one row, rather than one on top of another. You also may see additional toolbars, such as the Drawing toolbar.

If either toolbar is missing, or if other toolbars are displayed, perform the next steps.

To display or hide a toolbar:

1. Position the pointer over any visible toolbar and click the right mouse button. A shortcut menu appears. The menu lists all available toolbars and displays a check mark next to those currently displayed.

2. If the Standard or Formatting toolbar is not visible, click its name on the shortcut menu to place a check mark next to it. If any toolbars besides the Formatting and Standard toolbars have check marks, click each one to remove the check mark and hide the toolbar. Only the Standard and Formatting toolbars should be visible, as shown in Figure 1-6.

Figure 1-6	TWO TOOLBARS ON ONE ROW

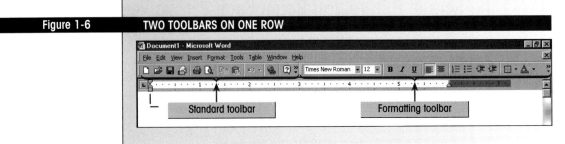

Standard toolbar

Formatting toolbar

If the toolbars appear on one row, as in Figure 1-6, perform the next steps to move the Formatting toolbar below the Standard toolbar.

To move the Formatting toolbar:

1. Click **Tools** on the menu bar, and then click **Customize**. The Customize dialog box opens.

   TROUBLE? If you don't see the Customize command on the Tools menu, point to the double-arrow, as explained earlier in this tutorial, to display the full list of commands.

2. Click the **Options** tab, and then click the **Standard and Formatting toolbars share one row** check box to remove the check.

3. Click **Close**. The Customize dialog box closes. The toolbars on your screen should now match those in Figure 1-3.

As you complete these tutorials, the ruler also should be visible to help you place items precisely.

To display the ruler:

1. Click **View** on the menu bar, and then point to the double-arrow at the bottom of the menu to display the hidden menu commands.

2. If "Ruler" does not have a check mark next to it, then click **Ruler**.

Setting the Font and Font Size

A **font** is a set of characters that has a certain design, shape, and appearance. Each font has a name, such as Courier, Times New Roman, or Arial. The **font size** is the actual height of a character, measured in points, where one point equals 1/72 of an inch in height. You'll learn more about fonts and font sizes later, but for now simply keep in mind that most of the documents you create will use the Times New Roman font in a font size of 12 points. Word usually uses a default (or predefined) setting of Times New Roman 12 point in new documents, but someone else might have changed the setting after Word was installed on your computer. You can see your computer's current settings in the Font list box, and the Font Size list box, in the Formatting toolbar, as shown in Figure 1-7.

| Figure 1-7 | DEFAULT FONT AND FONT SIZE SETTINGS |

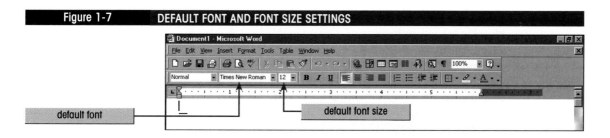

If your font setting is not Times New Roman 12 point, you should change the default setting now. You'll use the menu bar to choose the desired commands.

To change the default font and font size:

1. Click **Format** on the menu bar, and then click **Font** to open the Font dialog box. If necessary, click the Font tab. See Figure 1-8.

Figure 1-8   **FONT DIALOG BOX**

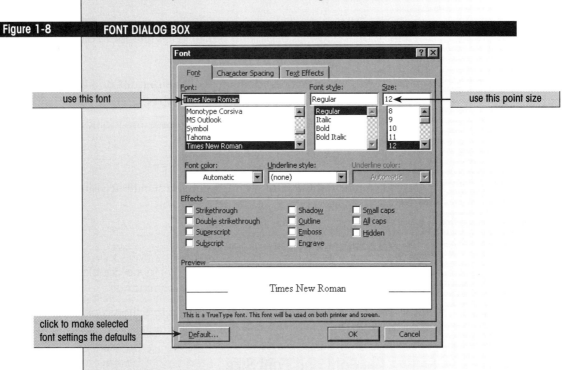

use this font

use this point size

click to make selected font settings the defaults

2. In the Font text box, click **Times New Roman**.

3. In the Size list box, click **12** to change the font to 12 point.

4. Click the **Default** button to make Times New Roman and 12 point the default settings. Word displays a message asking you to verify that you want to make 12-point Times New Roman the default font.

5. Click the **Yes** button.

Displaying Nonprinting Characters

Nonprinting characters are symbols that can be displayed on the screen but that do not show up when you print your document. You can display them when you are working on the appearance, or **format**, of your document. For example, one nonprinting character marks the end of a paragraph (¶), and another marks the space between words (•). It's sometimes helpful to display nonprinting characters so you can see whether you've typed an extra space, ended a paragraph, typed spaces instead of tabs, and so on. Generally, in these tutorials, you will display nonprinting characters only when you are formatting a document. You'll display them now, though, so you can use them as guides when typing your first letter.

To display nonprinting characters:

1. Click the Show/Hide ¶ button ¶ on the Standard toolbar. A paragraph mark (¶) appears at the top of the document window. See Figure 1-9.

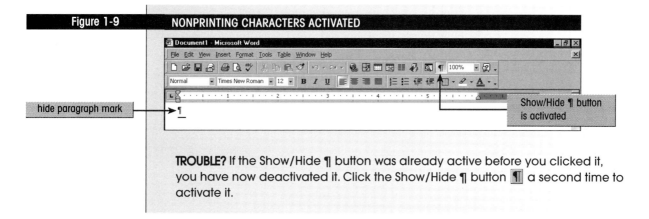

Figure 1-9   **NONPRINTING CHARACTERS ACTIVATED**

hide paragraph mark

Show/Hide ¶ button is activated

TROUBLE? If the Show/Hide ¶ button was already active before you clicked it, you have now deactivated it. Click the Show/Hide ¶ button ¶ a second time to activate it.

To make sure your screen always matches the figures in these tutorials, remember to complete the checklist in Figure 1-10 each time you sit down at the computer.

Figure 1-10   **WORD SCREEN SESSION CHECKLIST**

SCREEN ELEMENT	SETTING	CHECK
Document view	Normal view	☐
Word window	Maximized	☐
Standard toolbar	Displayed, below the menu bar	☐
Formatting toolbar	Displayed, below the Standard toolbar	☐
Other toolbars	Hidden	☐
Nonprinting characters	Hidden	☐
Font	Times New Roman	☐
Point size	12 point	☐
Ruler	Displayed	☐

Now that you have planned a document, opened the Word program, identified screen elements, and adjusted settings, you are ready to create a new document. In the next session, you will create Karen's letter to the Tacoma Chamber of Commerce.

Session 1.1 QUICK CHECK

1. In your own words, list and describe the steps in creating a document.

2. How do you start Word from the Windows desktop?

3. Define each of the following in your own words:

   a. nonprinting characters
   b. document view buttons
   c. font size
   d. default settings

4. How do you change the default font size?

5. How do you display or hide the Formatting toolbar?

6. How do you change the document view to normal view?

Typing a Letter

You're ready to type Karen's letter to the Tacoma Chamber of Commerce. Figure 1-11 shows the completed letter printed on the company letterhead. You'll begin by opening a new blank page (in case you accidentally typed something in the current page). Then you'll move the insertion point to about 2½ inches from the top margin of the paper to allow space for the Crossroads letterhead.

Figure 1-11   **JOB FAIR LETTER**

1414 East Bellingham S.W.
Suite 318
Tacoma, WA 98402

February 21, 2001

Deborah Brown, President
Tacoma Chamber of Commerce
210 Shoreline Vista, Suite 1103
Tacoma, WA 98402

Dear Deborah:

Recently, you contacted our staff about the Chamber's decision to sponsor a job fair again this year. We are interested in participating as we have done in the past.

Please send us information about the dates and location for this year's fair. If a map of the exhibit area is available, we would appreciate receiving a copy of it. Also, please send us the name and address of someone we can contact regarding the on-site physical facilities. Specifically, we need to know what size the exhibit booths are and how we can reserve one.

Thank you for your help in this matter. We look forward to participating in the job fair and hope to hear from you soon.

Sincerely yours,

Karen Liu
Executive Director

To open a new document:

1. If you took a break after the last session, make sure the Word program is running, that nonprinting characters are displayed, and that the font settings in the Formatting toolbar are set to 12-point Times New Roman. Also verify that the toolbars and the ruler are properly displayed.

2. Click the **New Blank Document** button [image] on the Standard toolbar to open a fresh document.

   If you have the taskbar displayed at the bottom of your screen, you see an additional button for the new document. If you wanted to switch back to Document1, you could simply click its button on the taskbar. Notice that the new document has only one set of Control menu buttons. When two or more documents are open, you click the Close button in the upper-right corner of the title bar to close that document. When only one document is open, you can click the Close Window button in the upper-right corner of the menu bar to close the document and leave Word open, or you can click the Close button in the upper-right corner of the title bar to close the document and exit Word.

3. Press the **Enter** key eight times. Each time you press the Enter key, a nonprinting paragraph mark appears. In the status bar (at the bottom of the document window), you should see the setting "At 2.5"," indicating that the insertion point is approximately 2½ inches from the top of the page. Another setting in the status bar should read "Ln 9," indicating the insertion point is in line 9 of the document. Note that your settings may be slightly different. See Figure 1-12.

Figure 1-12	DOCUMENT WINDOW AFTER INSERTING BLANK LINES

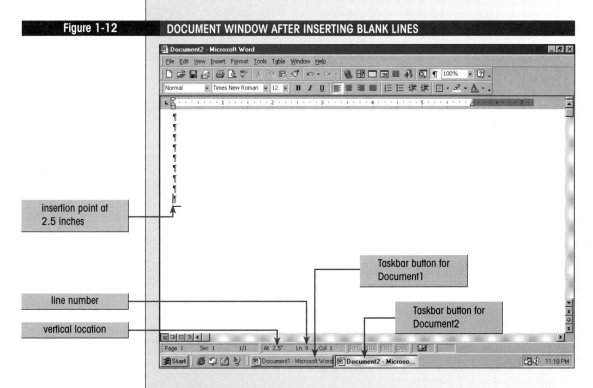

insertion point at 2.5 inches

Taskbar button for Document1

Taskbar button for Document2

line number

vertical location

TROUBLE? If the paragraph mark doesn't appear each time you press the Enter key, the nonprinting characters might be hidden. To show the nonprinting characters, click the Show/Hide ¶ button on the Standard toolbar, as described earlier in this tutorial.

> **TROUBLE?** If you pressed the Enter key too many times, press the Backspace key to delete each extra line and paragraph mark. If you're on line 9 but the "At" number is not 2.5", don't worry. Different monitors produce slightly different measurements when you press the Enter key.

Using AutoCompleteTips

Now you're ready to type the date. You'll take advantage of Word's **AutoComplete** feature, which automatically types dates and other regularly used words and text for you.

To insert the date using an AutoComplete tip:

1. Type **Febr** (the first four letters of February). An AutoComplete tip appears above the line, as shown in Figure 1-13. If you wanted to type something other than February, you would simply continue typing to complete the word. In this case, though, you want to accept the AutoComplete tip, so you will press the Enter key in the next step.

Figure 1-13	AUTOCOMPLETE TIP

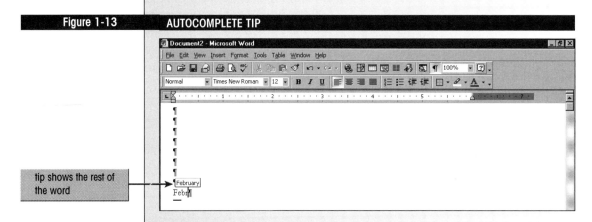

tip shows the rest of the word

> **TROUBLE?** If the AutoComplete tip doesn't appear, this feature may not be active. Click Tools on the menu bar, click AutoCorrect, click the AutoText tab, click the Show AutoComplete tip for AutoText and dates check box to insert a check, and then click OK.

2. Press the **Enter** key to insert the rest of the word "February."

3. Press the **spacebar** and then type **21, 2001** to complete the date. See Figure 1-14.

> **TROUBLE?** If February happens to be the current month, you will see an AutoComplete tip displaying the current date after you press the spacebar. To accept that AutoComplete tip, press Enter. Otherwise, simply type the rest of the date as instructed in Step 3.

Figure 1-14	DATE ENTERED IN THE DOCUMENT

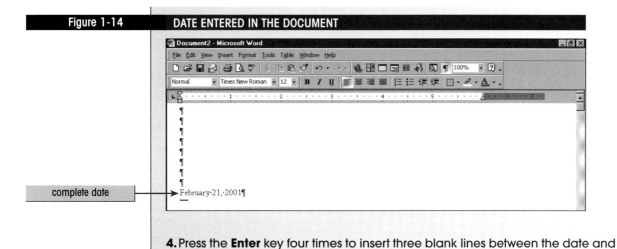

complete date

4. Press the **Enter** key four times to insert three blank lines between the date and the inside address. The status bar now should display "Ln13."

Next, you'll enter the inside address shown on Karen's note.

Entering Text

You'll enter the inside address by typing it. If you type a wrong character, simply press the Backspace key to delete the mistake and then retype it.

To type the inside address:

1. Type **Deborah Brown, President** and then press the **Enter** key. As you type, the nonprinting character (•) appears between words to indicate a space.

   TROUBLE? If a wavy red or green line appears beneath a word, check to make sure you typed the text correctly. If you did not, use the Backspace key to remove the error, and then retype the text correctly.

2. Type the following text, pressing the **Enter** key after each line to enter the inside address:

   Tacoma Chamber of Commerce
   210 Shoreline Vista, Suite 1103
   Tacoma, WA 98402

3. Press the **Enter** key again to add a blank line between the inside address and the salutation.

4. Type **Dear Deborah:** and press the **Enter** key twice to double space between the salutation and the body of the letter. When you press the Enter key the first time, the Office Assistant might appear, asking if you would like help writing your letter. Depending on the settings on your computer, you might see a different Office Assistant than the one shown in Figure 1-15.

Figure 1-15   **OFFICE ASSISTANT**

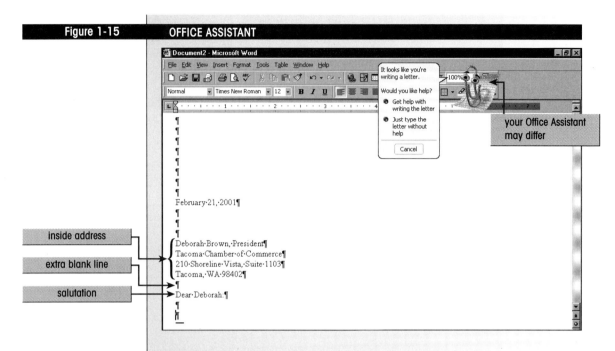

The Office Assistant is an interactive feature that sometimes appears to offer help on routine tasks. In this case, you could click the "Get help with writing the letter" button and have the Office Assistant lead you through a series of dialog boxes designed to set up the basic elements of your letter. You'll learn more about the Office Assistant later in this tutorial. For now, though, you'll close the Office Assistant and continue writing your letter.

5. Click the **Just type the letter without help** button to close the Office Assistant.

   TROUBLE? If the Office Assistant remains open, right-click the Office Assistant, and then click Hide to close it.

You have completed the date, the inside address, and the salutation of Karen's letter, using a standard business letter format. You're ready to complete the letter. Before you do, however, you should save what you have typed so far.

Saving a Document for the First Time

The letter on which you are working is stored only in the computer's memory, not on a disk. If you were to exit Word, turn off your computer, or experience an accidental power failure, the part of Karen's letter that you just typed would be lost. You should get in the habit of frequently saving your document to a disk.

The first time you save a document, you need to name it. The name you use is usually referred to as the **filename**. To make it easy for you to keep track of the various documents stored on your computer, or 3½-inch disk, or Zip disk, it's important to use names that accurately describe their contents. For example, if you use a generic name such as "Letter" for this particular document, you won't be able to differentiate it from other letters in the future. Instead, you should use a more descriptive name, such as Tacoma Job Fair Letter.

REFERENCE WINDOW **RW**

<u>Saving a Document for the First Time</u>
- Click the Save button on the Standard toolbar (or click File on the menu bar, and then click Save).
- If necessary, change the folder and drive information.
- In the File name text box, type the filename.
- Click the Save button (or press the Enter key).

After you name your document, Word automatically appends the .doc filename extension to identify the file as a Microsoft Word document. However, depending on how Windows is set up on your computer, you might not actually see the .doc extension. These tutorials assume that filename extensions are hidden.

To save the document:

1. Place your Data Disk in the appropriate disk drive.

   TROUBLE? If you don't have a Data Disk, you need to get one before you can proceed. Your instructor or technical support person will either give you one or ask you to make your own by following the instructions on the "Read This Before You Begin" page at the beginning of this tutorial. See your instructor or technical support person for more information.

2. Click the **Save** button 🖫 on the Standard toolbar. The Save As dialog box opens. See Figure 1-16. Note that Word suggests using the first few characters of the letter ("February 21") as the filename. You will replace the suggested filename with something more descriptive.

Figure 1-16	SAVE AS DIALOG BOX

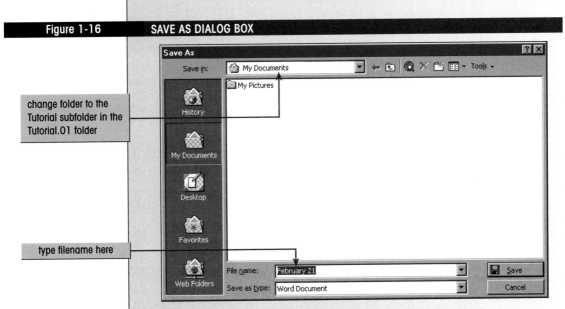

change folder to the Tutorial subfolder in the Tutorial.01 folder

type filename here

3. Type **Tacoma Job Fair Letter** in the File name text box.

4. Click the **Save in** list arrow, click the drive containing your Data Disk, double-click the **Tutorial.01** folder, then double-click the **Tutorial** folder. The Tutorial folder is now open and ready for you to save the document. See Figure 1-17.

| Figure 1-17 | SAVE AS DIALOG BOX WITH TUTORIAL FOLDER OPEN |

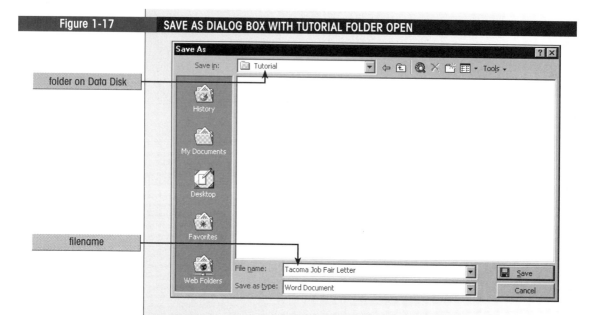

TROUBLE? If Word automatically adds the .doc extension to your filename, then your computer is configured to show filename extensions. Just continue with the tutorial.

5. Click the **Save** button in the Save As dialog box. The dialog box closes, and you return to the document window. The name of your file appears in the title bar.

Adding Properties to a Document

After you save a document, you should record some descriptive information in a special dialog box known as the document's **properties page**. The information that you record here is known, collectively, as a document's **properties**. For example, you might include your name and a description of the document. Later, you or one of your co-workers can review the document's properties for a quick summary of its purpose, without having to skim the entire document. You'll look at the properties page for the Tacoma Job Fair Letter next.

To view the properties page for the Tacoma Job Fair Letter document:

1. Click **File** on the menu bar, click **Properties**, and then, if necessary, click the **Summary** tab. The Tacoma Job Fair Letter Properties dialog box opens, as shown in Figure 1-18.

Figure 1-18 | **PROPERTIES PAGE FOR THE ACTIVE DOCUMENT**

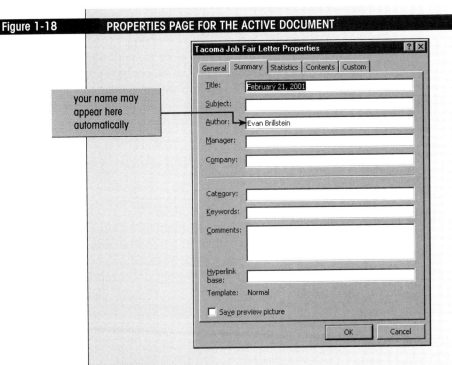

your name may
appear here
automatically

TROUBLE? If you don't see the Properties command on the File menu, point to the double-arrow to display the hidden menu commands.

This dialog box takes its name from the active document (in this case, "Tacoma Job Fair Letter"). Depending on how your computer is set up, the Author text box already may contain your name or the name of the registered owner of your copy of Word. In addition, the Title text box may contain the document's first line of text, "February 21, 2001." Because you already have assigned a descriptive name to this file ("Tacoma Job Fair Letter"), there's no reason to include a title here. You can delete this title and then enter relevant information in the appropriate text boxes. The Comments text box is a good place to record useful notes about the document, such as its purpose.

To edit the contents of the properties page:

1. Verify that the text in the Title text box is highlighted, and then press the **Delete** key.

2. Press the **Tab** key twice. The insertion point moves to the Author text box.

3. If necessary, type your name in the Author text box.

4. Click the Comments text box, and then type **A letter requesting information on the job fair.**

5. Click **OK**. The Tacoma Job Fair Letter dialog box closes, and the document's new properties are saved.

It's good practice to add information to a document's properties page right after you save the document for the first time. You will find such information useful once you have accumulated a number of Word documents and want to organize them. You can use the properties to find documents quickly. As you will see in the Review Assignments at the end of this tutorial, you can view a document's properties page without actually opening the document.

Word Wrap

Now that you have saved your document and its properties, you're ready to complete Karen's letter. As you type the body of the letter, do not press the Enter key at the end of each line. When you type a word that extends into the right margin, both the insertion point and the word move automatically to the next line. This automatic line breaking is called **word wrap**. You'll see how word wrap works as you type the body of Karen's letter.

To observe word wrap while typing a paragraph:

1. Make sure the insertion point is at Ln 20 Col 1 (according to the settings in the status bar). If it's not, move it to that location by pressing the arrow keys.

2. Type the following sentence slowly and watch when the insertion point jumps to the next line: **Recently, you contacted our staff about the Chamber's decision to sponsor a job fair again this year.** Notice how Word moves the last few words to a new line when the previous one is full. See Figure 1-19.

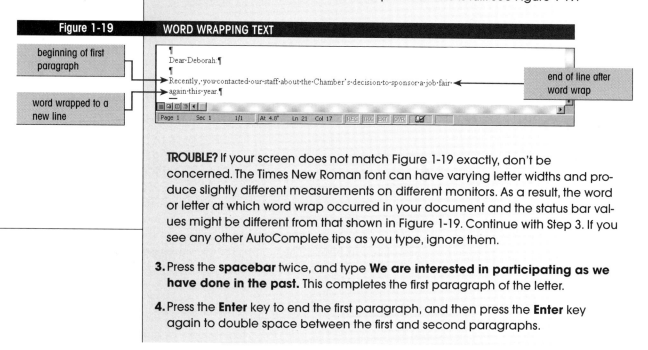

| Figure 1-19 | WORD WRAPPING TEXT |

beginning of first paragraph

word wrapped to a new line

end of line after word wrap

TROUBLE? If your screen does not match Figure 1-19 exactly, don't be concerned. The Times New Roman font can have varying letter widths and produce slightly different measurements on different monitors. As a result, the word or letter at which word wrap occurred in your document and the status bar values might be different from that shown in Figure 1-19. Continue with Step 3. If you see any other AutoComplete tips as you type, ignore them.

3. Press the **spacebar** twice, and type **We are interested in participating as we have done in the past.** This completes the first paragraph of the letter.

4. Press the **Enter** key to end the first paragraph, and then press the **Enter** key again to double space between the first and second paragraphs.

Scrolling a Document

After you finish the last set of steps, the insertion point will be at or near the bottom of your document window. It might seem that no room is left in the document window to type the rest of Karen's letter. However, as you continue to add text at the end of your document, the text that you typed earlier will **scroll** (or shift up) and disappear from the top of the document window. You'll see how scrolling works as you enter the final text of Karen's letter.

To observe scrolling while you're entering text:

1. Make sure the insertion point is at the bottom of the screen, to the left of the second paragraph mark in the body of the letter.

> **TROUBLE?** If you are using a very large monitor, your insertion point may still be some distance from the bottom of the screen. In that case, you may not be able to perform the scrolling steps that follow. Simply read the steps to familiarize yourself with the process of scrolling. You'll scroll longer documents later.
>
> **2.** Type the second paragraph, as shown in Figure 1-20, and then press the **Enter** key twice to insert a blank line. Notice that as you type the paragraph, the top of the letter scrolls off the top of the document window. Don't worry if you make a mistake in your typing. You'll learn a number of ways to correct errors in the next section.
>
> **TROUBLE?** If you have difficulty reading the text in Figure 1-20, refer back to Figure 1-11.

Figure 1-20	TOP OF THE LETTER SCROLLED OFF THE SCREEN

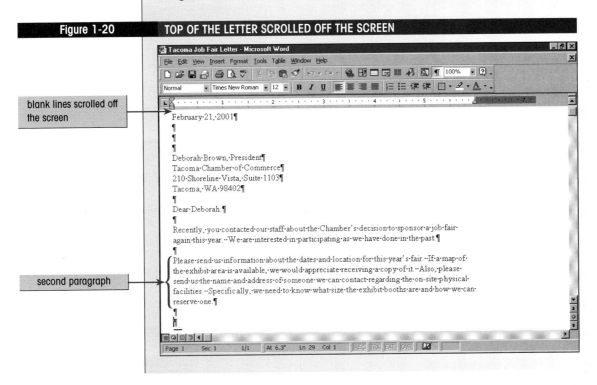

Correcting Errors

Have you made any typing mistakes yet? If so, don't worry. The advantage of using a word processor is that you can correct mistakes quickly and efficiently. Word provides several ways to correct errors when you're entering text.

If you discover a typing error as soon as you make it, you can press the Backspace key to erase the characters and spaces to the left of the insertion point one at a time. Backspacing will erase both printing and nonprinting characters. After you erase the error, you can type the correct characters.

Word also provides a feature, called **AutoCorrect**, that checks for errors in your document as you type and automatically corrects common typing errors, such as "adn" for "and." If the spelling of a particular word differs from its spelling in the Word electronic dictionary, or if a word isn't in the dictionary at all (for example, a person's name), a wavy *red* line appears beneath the word. A wavy red line also appears if you type duplicate words (such as "the the"). If you accidentally type an extra space between words or make a grammatical error (such as typing "He walk to the store." instead of "He walks to the store."), a wavy *green* line appears beneath the error. You'll see how AutoCorrect works when you intentionally make typing errors.

To correct common typing errors:

1. Carefully and slowly type the following sentence exactly as it is shown, including the spelling errors and the extra space between the last two words: **Word corects teh commen typing misTakes you make.** Press the **Enter** key when you are finished typing. Notice that as you press the spacebar after the word "commen," a wavy red line appears beneath it, indicating that the word might be misspelled. Notice also that when you pressed the spacebar after the words "corects," "teh," and "misTakes," Word automatically corrected the spelling. After you pressed the Enter key, a wavy green line appeared under the last two words, alerting you to the extra space. See Figure 1-21.

Figure 1-21	DOCUMENT WINDOW SHOWING TYPING ERRORS

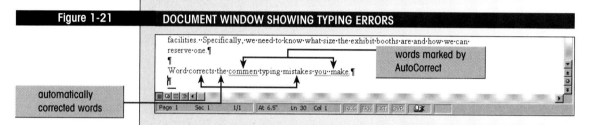

TROUBLE? If red and green wavy lines do not appear beneath mistakes, Word is probably not set to automatically check spelling and grammar as you type. Click Tools on the menu bar, and then click Options to open the Options dialog box. Click the Spelling & Grammar tab. Make sure there are check marks in the Check spelling as you type and the Check grammar as you type check boxes, and click OK. If Word does not automatically correct the incorrect spelling of "the," click Tools on the menu bar, click AutoCorrect, and make sure that all five boxes at the top of the AutoCorrect tab have check marks. Then scroll down the AutoCorrect list to make sure that there is an entry that changes "teh" to "the," and click OK.

2. Position the I-Beam pointer $\rm I$ over the word "commen" and click the right mouse button. A list box appears with suggested spellings. See Figure 1-22.

Figure 1-22	LIST BOX SHOWING AUTOCORRECT SUGGESTED SPELLINGS

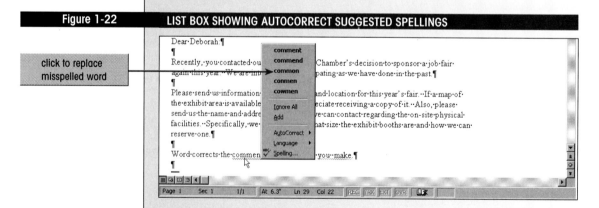

TROUBLE? If the list box doesn't appear, repeat Step 2, making sure you click the right mouse button, not the left one.

3. Click **common** in the list box. The list box disappears, and the correct spelling appears in your document. Notice that the wavy red line disappears after you correct the error.

4. Click to the right of the letter "u" in the word "you." Press the **Delete** key to delete the extra space.

You can see how quick and easy it is to correct common typing errors with AutoCorrect. Remember, however, that there is no substitute for your own eyes. You should thoroughly proofread each document you create, keeping in mind that AutoCorrect will not catch words that are spelled correctly, but used improperly (such as "your" for "you're"). Proofread your document now, and use AutoCorrect or the Backspace or Delete keys to correct any mistakes.

Before you continue typing Karen's letter, you'll need to delete your practice sentence.

To delete the practice sentence:

1. Click between the period and the paragraph mark at the end of the sentence.

2. Press and hold the **Backspace** key until the entire sentence is deleted. Then press the **Delete** key to delete the extra paragraph mark.

3. Make sure the insertion point is in line 29. There should be one nonprinting paragraph mark between the second paragraph and the paragraph you will type next.

Finishing **the Letter**

You're ready to complete the rest of the letter. As you type, you can use any of the techniques you learned in the previous section to correct mistakes.

To complete the letter:

1. Type the final paragraph of the body of the letter, as shown in Figure 1-23, and then press the **Enter** key twice. Accept or ignore AutoComplete tips as necessary. Unless you have a very large monitor, the date and, possibly, part of the inside address scroll off the top of the document window completely.

Figure 1-23	FINAL PARAGRAPH

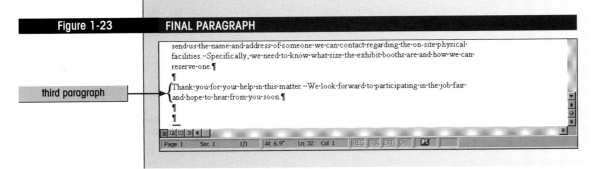

third paragraph

2. Type **Sincerely yours,** (including the comma) to enter the complimentary close.

3. Press the **Enter** key four times to allow space for your signature.

4. Type your name. See Figure 1-24.

Figure 1-24	COMPLIMENTARY CLOSING OF LETTER

reserve·one.¶
¶
Thank·you·for·your·help·in·this·matter.··We·look·forward·to·participating·in·the·job·fair·
and·hope·to·hear·from·you·soon.¶
¶
Sincerely·Yours,¶
¶
¶
¶
Evan·Brillstein¶

Page 1   Sec 1   1/1   At 7.7"   Ln 36 Col 16   REC TRK EXT OVR

In the last set of steps, you watched the text at the top of your document move off your screen. You can scroll this hidden text back into view so you can read the beginning of the letter. When you do, the text at the bottom of the screen will scroll out of view.

To scroll the text using the scroll bar:

1. Position the mouse pointer on the up arrow at the top of the vertical scroll bar. Press and hold the mouse button to scroll the text. When the text stops scrolling, you have reached the top of the document and can see the beginning of the letter. Note that scrolling does not change the location of the insertion point in the document.

If you wanted to view the end of the letter, you would use the down arrow at the bottom of the vertical scroll bar. Because you have completed the letter, you'll save the document.

Saving a Completed Document

Although you saved the letter earlier, the text that you typed since then exists only in the computer's memory. That means you need to save your document again. It's especially important to save your document before printing. Then, if you experience problems that cause your computer to stop working while you are printing, you will still have on your disk a copy of the document containing your most recent additions and changes.

To save the completed letter:

1. Make sure your Data Disk is still in the appropriate disk drive.

2. Click the **Save** button 🖫 on the Standard toolbar. Because you named and saved this file earlier, you can save the document without being prompted for information. Word saves your letter with the same name and to the same location you specified earlier.

Previewing and Printing a Document

The current document window displays the text, but you cannot see an entire page without scrolling. To see how the page will look when printed, you need to use the Print Preview window.

To preview the document:

1. Click the **Print Preview** button 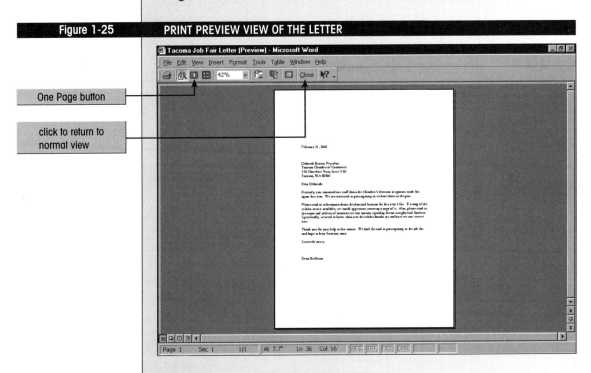 on the Standard toolbar. The Print Preview window opens and displays a full-page version of your letter, as shown in Figure 1-25. This shows how the letter will fit on the printed page.

Figure 1-25	PRINT PREVIEW VIEW OF THE LETTER

One Page button

click to return to normal view

TROUBLE? If your letter in the Print Preview window is smaller and off to the left rather than centered in the window, click the One Page button on the Print Preview toolbar.

TROUBLE? If you see rulers above and to the left of the document, your rulers are displayed. You can hide the rulers in Print Preview by clicking the View Rulers button on the Print Preview toolbar.

2. Click the **Close** button on the Print Preview toolbar to return to normal view.

Note that you should always preview a document before printing. That way, you can correct problems without wasting paper on an imperfect document. It's especially important to preview documents if your computer is connected to a network so that you don't keep a shared printer tied up with unnecessary printing. In this case, the text looks well-spaced and the letterhead will fit at the top of the page. You're ready to print the letter.

When printing a document, you have two choices. You can use the Print command on the File menu, which opens the Print dialog box in which you can adjust some printer settings. Also, you can use the Print button on the Standard toolbar, which simply prints the document using default settings, without displaying a dialog box. In each session of these tutorials, the first time you print from a shared computer, you should check the settings in the Print dialog box and make sure the number of copies is set to one. After that, you can use the Print button.

To print a document:

1. Make sure your printer is turned on and contains paper.

2. Click **File** on the menu bar, and then click **Print**. The Print dialog box opens. See Figure 1-26.

Figure 1-26   PRINT DIALOG BOX

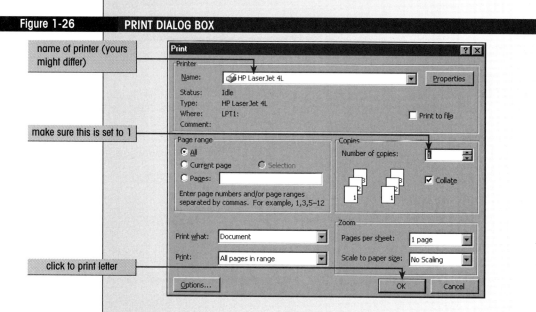

3. Verify that your settings match those in Figure 1-26. In particular, make sure the number of copies is set to 1. Also make sure the Printer section of the dialog box shows the correct printer. If you're not sure what the correct printer is, check with your instructor or technical support person.

   TROUBLE? If the Print dialog box shows the wrong printer, click the Printer Name list arrow, and then select the correct printer from the list of available printers.

4. Click the **OK** button to print Karen's letter. A printer icon 🖨 appears at the far right of the taskbar to indicate that your document is being sent to the printer.

Your printed letter should look similar to Figure 1-11 but without the Crossroads letterhead. The word wraps, or line breaks, might not appear in the same places on your letter because the size and spacing of characters vary slightly from one printer to the next.

Karen also needs an envelope to mail her letter in. Printing an envelope is easy in Word. You'll have a chance to try it in the Review Assignments at the end of this tutorial. If you wanted to find out how to print an envelope yourself, you could use the Word Help system.

Getting **Help**

The Word Help system provides quick access to information about commands, features, and screen elements.

The **What's This?** command on the Help menu provides context-sensitive Help information. When you choose this command, the pointer changes to the Help pointer ↳**?**, which you can then use to click any object or option on the screen, including menu commands, to see a description of the item.

You've already encountered another form of help, the animated Office Assistant. The **Office Assistant** is an interactive guide to finding information on Microsoft Word. As you learned earlier in this tutorial, the Office Assistant sometimes opens automatically to help you with routine tasks. You also can ask the Office Assistant a direction question, and it will search the Help system to find an answer in plain English. The Office Assistant is a context-sensitive tool, which means that it is designed to offer information related to your current task. If you simply want to look up some information in Word's Help system, as you would in an Encyclopedia, you can use the Index and Contents tabs. You will learn how to use the Office Assistant as well as to display the Index and Contents tabs in the following steps.

REFERENCE WINDOW   **RW**

Getting Help from the Office Assistant
- Click the Microsoft Word Help button on the Standard toolbar (or click Help on the menu bar and then click Microsoft Word Help).
- Type your question, and then click the Search button.
- Click a topic from the list of topics displayed.
- Read the information in the Microsoft Word Help window. For more information, click the relevant underlined text.
- To display the Index or Contents tab, click the Show button in the Microsoft Word Help window. Click the Hide button to hide these tabs.
- To close the Microsoft Word Help window, click its Close button.
- To hide the Office Assistant, click Help on the menu bar, and then click Hide the Office Assistant.

You'll use the Office Assistant now to learn how to print an envelope.

To use the Office Assistant to learn how to print an envelope:

1. Click the **Microsoft Word Help** button [?] on the Standard toolbar. The Office Assistant opens, offering help on topics related to the task you most recently performed (if any), and asking what you'd like to do. The Office Assistant shown in Figure 1-27 takes the form of an animated paperclip, but your Office Assistant may differ.

Figure 1-27	OFFICE ASSISTANT

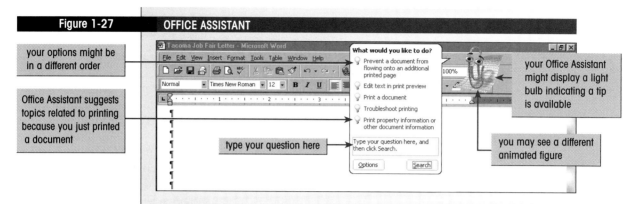

your options might be in a different order

Office Assistant suggests topics related to printing because you just printed a document

type your question here

your Office Assistant might display a light bulb indicating a tip is available

you may see a different animated figure

2. Type **How do I print an envelope?** and then click the **Search** button. The Office Assistant window shows topics related to envelopes.

TROUBLE? If you do not see a space to type a question, click the Help with something else option button, and then continue with Step 2.

3. Click **Create and print envelopes.** The Microsoft Word Help window opens next to or on top of the Word window, with even more specific topics related to printing envelopes.

4. Click **Create and print an envelope.** The Microsoft Word Help window displays the precise steps involved in printing an envelope. See Figure 1-28. To scroll through the steps, drag the vertical scroll bar. Note that within a Help window, you can click on underlined text to display more information.

Figure 1-28	STEPS FOR PRINTING AN ENVELOPE

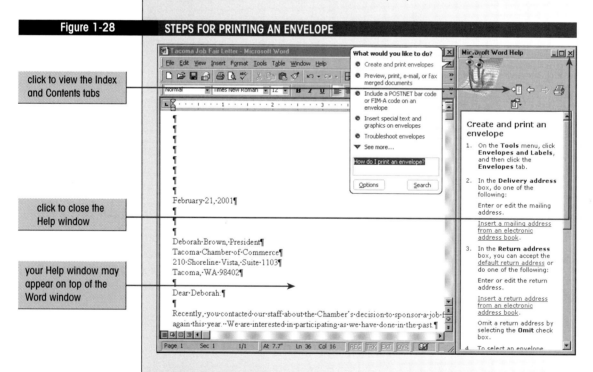

click to view the Index and Contents tabs

click to close the Help window

your Help window may appear on top of the Word window

TROUBLE? If your Help window doesn't exactly match the one in Figure 1-28, just continue with these steps. You will learn how to display and hide additional tabs of the Help Window shortly.

5. Click the **Show** button 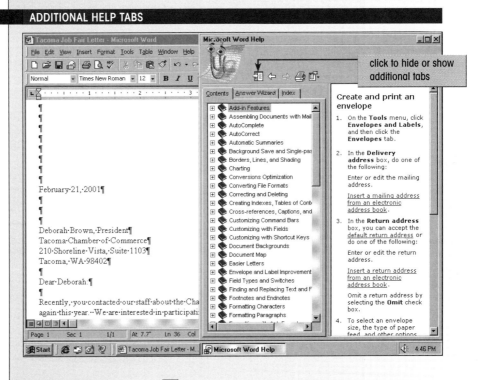. Additional Help window tabs appear, as in Figure 1-29. The most useful of these are the Contents tab (where you can search by general topics) and the Index tab (where you can look up a specific entry). You will have a chance to practice using these tabs in the Review Assignments at the end of this tutorial.

Figure 1-29	ADDITIONAL HELP TABS

6. Click the **Hide** button to return the Help window to its original size.

7. Click the **Close** button ✕ on the Microsoft Word Help window. The Microsoft Word Help window closes, and the Word program window fills the screen again.

8. Click **Help** on the menu bar, and then click **Hide the Office Assistant**. The animated Office Assistant disappears.

TROUBLE? If the Office Assistant asks if you want to hide it permanently, choose the "No just hide me" option.

Some Help windows have different formats than those you've just seen. However, they all provide the information you need to complete any task in Word.

Exiting Word

You have now finished typing and printing the letter to the Tacoma Chamber of Commerce, and you are ready to **exit**, or quit, Word. When you exit Word, you close both the document and the program window.

> **REFERENCE WINDOW**   **RW**
>
> Exiting Word
> - Click the Close button for each open document (or click File on the menu bar, and then click Exit).
> - If you're prompted to save changes to the document, click the Yes button; then, if necessary, type a document name and click the Save button.

Because you've completed the first draft of Karen's letter, you can close the document window and exit Word now.

> ### *To close documents and exit Word:*
>
> **1.** Click the **Close** button ❎ in the title bar to close the letter.
>
> **TROUBLE?** If you see a dialog box with the message "Do you want to save the changes you made to Tacoma Job Fair Letter?," you have made changes to the document since the last time you saved it. Click the Yes button to save the current version and close it.
>
> **2.** Click the **Close Window** button ❎ on the right side of the menu bar to close the blank Document1.
>
> **TROUBLE?** If you see a dialog box with the message "Do you want to save the changes you made to Document1?," click the No button.
>
> **3.** Click the **Close** button ❎ in the upper-right corner of the Word window. Word closes, and you return to the Windows desktop.

You give the letter for the Tacoma Chamber of Commerce to Karen for her to review. Now that you have created and saved your letter, you are ready to learn about editing and formatting a document in the next tutorial.

Session 1.2 QUICK | CHECK

1. Explain how to save a document for the first time.

2. What is the advantage of recording information about a document in its Properties dialog box?

3. Explain how word wrap works in a Word document.

4. What is the Office Assistant, and how do you use it?

5. In your own words, define each of the following:

   a. scrolling
   b. AutoComplete
   c. AutoCorrect
   d. print preview

6. Describe two methods for exiting Word.

REVIEW ASSIGNMENTS

Karen received a response from the Tacoma Chamber of Commerce containing the information she requested about the job fair, and Crossroads has firmed up its plans to participate as an exhibitor. Karen must now staff the booth with Crossroads employees for each day of the five-day fair. She sends a memo to employees asking them to commit to two dates. Create the memo shown in Figure 1-30 by completing the following:

1. If necessary, start Word and make sure your Data Disk is in the appropriate disk drive, and then check your screen to make sure your settings match those in the tutorials.

2. If the Office Assistant is open, hide it by using the appropriate command on the Help menu.

3. Click the New Blank Document button on the Standard toolbar to display a new document.

4. Press the Enter key six times to insert approximately 2 inches of space before the memo headings.

5. Press the Caps Lock key, and then type "MEMORANDUM" (without the quotation marks) in capital letters.

6. Press the Enter key twice, type "TO:" (without the quotation marks), press the Caps Lock key to turn off capitalization, press the Tab key three times, and then type "Crossroads Staff Members" (without the quotation marks).

7. Press the Enter key twice, type "FROM:" (without the quotation marks), press the Tab key twice, and then type your name. Throughout the rest of this exercise, use the Caps Lock Key as necessary to turn capitalization on and off.

Explore

8. Press the Enter key twice, type "DATE:" (without the quotation marks), press the Tab key three times. Insert today's date from your computer clock by clicking Insert on the menu bar, clicking Date and Time, clicking the date format that corresponds to June 16, 2001, and then clicking OK.

9. Continue typing the rest of the memo exactly as shown in Figure 1-30, including any misspellings and extra words. Notice how Word automatically corrects some misspellings. (You will have a chance to practice correcting the remaining errors later.) Press the Tab key twice after "SUBJECT:" to align the memo heading evenly. Include two blank lines between the Subject line and the body of the memo.

Figure 1-30   **SAMPLE MEMO**

MEMORANDUM

TO: Crossroads Staff Members

FROM: Karen Liu

DATE: June 16, 2001

SUBJECT: Dates for 2001 Job Fair

The the 2001 Job Fair sponsored by the Tacoma Chamber of Commerce will be held
October 20-25, 2001,from 11:00 a.m. to 5:00 p.m.. This fiar provvides us with an
oportunity to inform Tacoma residents about our services. Previously, we have each spent
two days helping at the exhibet. Please let me know which days you would prefer this
year. I would like this information by tomorrow.

Thanks for your help.

10. Save your work as **Job Fair Reminder Memo** in the Review folder for Tutorial 1.

11. Click File on the menu bar, and then click Properties. Delete the existing title for the document, verify that your name appears in the Author text box, and type a brief description of the document in the Comments text box. Click OK to close the document's properties page.

12. Correct the misspelled words, indicated by the wavy red lines. If the correct version of a word does not appear in the list box, press the Escape key to close the list, and then make the correction yourself. To ignore an AutoCorrect suggestion, click Ignore All. Then correct any grammatical or other errors indicated by wavy green lines. Use the Backspace key to delete any extra words or spaces.

13. Scroll to the beginning of the memo. Click at the beginning of the first line and insert room for the letterhead by pressing the Enter key until MEMORANDUM is at line 12.

14. Save your most recent changes.

Explore ▷ 15. Use the What's This? feature to learn about the Word Count command on the Tools menu. Click Help on the menu bar, and then click What's This? Click Tools on the menu bar, click Word Count, and then read the text box. When you are finished, click the text box to close it.

16. Preview and print the memo.

17. Use the Office Assistant to open a Microsoft Word Help menu with the steps necessary for printing an address on an envelope.

Explore ▷ 18. With the Help window open on one side of the screen, and the Word window open on the other, follow the instructions for printing an envelope. (Check with your instructor or technical support person to make sure you can print envelopes. If not, print on an 8½ x 11-inch sheet of paper.) To place the Help and Word windows side by side, right-click the taskbar and then click Tile Windows Vertically. When you are done, right-click the taskbar and then click Undo Tile.

Explore 19. With the Help window open, click the Show button, if necessary, to display the additional Help tabs. Click the Index tab, type "Help" (without the quotation marks) and then click the Search button. View the topics related to Word's Help system in the Choose a topic list box. Click any topic in the right-hand window to read more about it. Next, click the Contents tab, review the main topics on that tab, and then click any plus sign to display subtopics. Click a subtopic to display additional topics in the right-hand window, then click one of those topics to display even more information. Continue to explore the Contents and Index tabs. When you are finished, close the Microsoft Word Help window. Hide the Office Assistant.

20. Close the document without saving your most recent changes.

21. Click the Open button on the Standard toolbar.

Explore 22. Verify that the Review folder for Tutorial 1 is displayed in the Look in list box, right-click the Job Fair Reminder Memo, and then click Properties in the shortcut menu. Review the document's properties page. You can use this technique to find out about the contents of a document quickly, without opening the document. Click OK to close the document's properties page, and then click Cancel to close the Open dialog box.

23. Close any open documents.

CASE PROBLEMS

Case 1. Letter to Confirm a Conference Date As catering director for the Madison Convention and Visitors Bureau, you are responsible for managing food service at the convention center. The Southern Wisconsin chapter of the National Purchasing Management Association has requested a written confirmation of a daily breakfast buffet during its annual convention scheduled for July 6-10, 2001.

Create the letter using the skills you learned in the tutorial. Remember to include today's date, the inside address, the salutation, the date of the reservation, the complimentary close, and your name and title. If the instructions show quotation marks around text you type, do not include the quotation marks in your letter. To complete the letter, do the following:

1. If necessary, start Word, make sure your Data Disk is in the appropriate disk drive, and check your screen to make sure your settings match those in the tutorials.

2. Open a new, blank document and press the Enter key until the insertion point is positioned about 2 inches from the top of the page. (Remember that you can see the exact position of the insertion point, in inches, in the status bar.)

Explore 3. Begin typing today's date. If an AutoComplete tip appears to finish the month, press Enter to accept it. Press the spacebar. If another AutoComplete tip appears with the rest of the date, press Enter to accept it. Otherwise, continue typing the date.

4. Press the Enter key six times after the date, and, using the proper business letter format, type the inside address: "Charles Quade, 222 Sydney Street, Whitewater, WI 57332."

5. Double space after the inside address (that is, press the Enter key twice), type the salutation "Dear Mr. Quade:," and then double space again. If the Office Assistant opens, click Cancel to close it.

6. Write one paragraph confirming the daily breakfast buffets for July 6-10, 2001.

7. Double space and type the complimentary close "Sincerely," (include the comma).

8. Press the Enter key four times to leave room for the signature, and then type your name and title.

9. Save the letter as **Confirmation Letter** in the Cases folder for Tutorial 1.

10. Use the document's properties page to record your name and a brief summary of the document.

11. Reread your letter carefully, and correct any errors.

12. Save any new changes.

13. Preview and print the letter.

14. Close the document.

Case 2. *Letter to Request Information about a "Climbing High" Franchise* You are the manager of the UpTown Sports Mall and are interested in obtaining a franchise for "Climbing High," an indoor rock-climbing venture marketed by Ultimate Sports, Inc. After reading an advertisement for the franchise, you decide to write for more information.

Create the letter by doing the following:

1. If necessary, start Word, make sure your Data Disk is in the appropriate disk drive, and check your screen to make sure your settings match those in the tutorials.

2. Open a new blank document, and press the Enter key until the insertion point is positioned about 2 inches from the top of the page. (Remember that you can see the exact position of the insertion point, in inches, in the status bar.)

3. Use AutoComplete (as described in Step 3 of the previous case project) to type today's date at the insertion point.

4. Press the Enter key six times after the date, and, using the proper business letter format, type the inside address: "Ultimate Sports, Inc., 2124 Martin Luther King Jr. Avenue, Rockton, CO 80911."

5. Insert a blank line after the inside address, type the salutation "Dear Franchise Manager:," and then insert another blank line.

6. Type the first paragraph as follows: "I'd like some information about the Climbing High indoor rock-climbing franchise. As manager of UpTown Sports Mall, a large sporting goods store, I've had success with similar programs, including both bungee jumping and snowboarding franchises."(Do not include the quotation marks.)

7. Save your work as **Rock Climbing Request Letter** in the Cases folder for Tutorial 1.

8. Use the document's properties page to record your name and a brief summary of the document.

Explore

9. Insert one blank line, and type the following: "Please answer the following questions:". Then press the Enter key, and type these questions on separate lines: "How much does your franchise cost?" "Does the price include the cost for installing the 30-foot simulated rock wall illustrated in your advertisement?" "Does the price include the cost for purchasing the ropes and harnesses?" Open the Office Assistant, type the question, "How can I add bullets to lists?," click the Search button, and then click the "Add bullets to lists" topic. In the Microsoft Word Help window, click the "Add bullets or numbering" subtopic, and then follow the instructions to insert a bullet in front of each question in the document. Close the Office Assistant and the Microsoft Word Help window when you are finished.

10. Correct any typing errors indicated by wavy lines. (*Hint:* Because "UpTown" is spelled correctly, click Ignore All on the shortcut menu to remove the wavy red line under the word "UpTown" and prevent Word from marking the word as a misspelling.)

11. Insert another blank line at the end of the letter, and type the complimentary close "Sincerely," (include the comma).

12. Press the Enter key four times to leave room for the signature, and type your full name and title. Then press the Enter key and type "UpTown Sports Mall." Notice that UpTown is not marked as a spelling error this time.

13. Save the letter with changes.

14. Preview the letter using the Print Preview button.

15. Print the letter.

16. Close the document.

Case 3. Memo of Congratulations Judy Davidoff is owner, founder, and president of Blossoms Unlimited, a chain of garden stores. She was recently honored by the Southern Council of Organic Gardeners for her series of free public seminars on organic vegetable gardening. Also, she was named businesswoman of the year by the Georgia Women's Business Network. Do the following:

1. If necessary, start Word, make sure your Data Disk is in the appropriate disk drive, and check your screen to make sure your settings match those in the tutorials.

2. Write a brief memo congratulating Judy on receiving these awards. Remember to use the four-part planning process. You should plan the content, organization, and style of the memo, and use a standard memo format similar to the one shown in Figure 1-30.

3. Save the document as **Awards Memo** in the Cases folder for Tutorial 1.

4. Use the document's properties page to record your name and a brief summary of the document.

5. Preview and print the memo.

6. Close the document.

Explore

Case 4. Writing a Personal Letter with the Letter Template Word provides templates— that is, models with predefined formatting—to help you create documents quickly and effectively. For example, the Letter template helps you create letters with professional-looking letterheads and with various letter formats. Do the following:

1. If necessary, start Word, make sure your Data Disk is in the appropriate disk drive, and check your screen to make sure your settings match those in the tutorials.

2. Click File on the menu bar, and then click New. The New dialog box opens.

3. Click the Letters & Faxes tab, click Elegant Letter, and then click the OK button. A letter template opens, as shown in Figure 1-31, containing generic, placeholder text that you can replace with your own information.

Figure 1-31 **ELEGANT LETTER TEMPLATE**

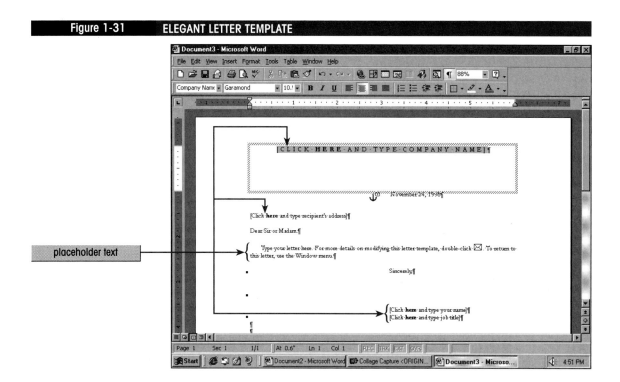

4. Click the line "CLICK HERE AND TYPE COMPANY NAME" (at the top of the document), and type the name of your school or company.

5. Click the line "Click here and type recipient's address," and type a real or fictitious name and address.

6. Delete the placeholder text in the body of the letter, and replace it with a sentence or two explaining that you're using the Word letter template to create this letter.

7. At the end of the letter, replace the placeholder text with your name and job title.

8. At the bottom of the page, replace the placeholder text with your address, phone number, and fax number. (Use fictious information if you prefer.)

9. Save the letter as **My Template Letter** (in the Cases folder for Tutorial 1), and then print it.

10. Use the document's properties page to record your name and a brief summary of the document.

11. Close the document.

LAB ASSIGNMENTS

The New Perspectives Labs are designed to help you master some of the key computer concepts and skills presented in each chapter of the text. If you are using your school's lab computers, your instructor or technical support person should have installed the Labs software for you. If you want to use the Labs on your home computer, ask your instructor for the appropriate software. See the Read This Before You Begin page for more information on installing and starting the Lab.

Each Lab has two parts: Steps and Explore. Use Steps first to learn and review concepts. Read the information on each page and do the numbered steps. As you work through the Lab, you will be asked to answer Quick Check questions about what you have learned. At the end of the Lab, you will see a Summary Report of your answers to the Quick Checks. If your instructor wants you to turn in this Summary Report, click the Print button on the Summary Report screen.

When you have completed the Steps, you can click the Explore button to complete the Lab Assignments. You also can use Explore to practice the skills you learned and to explore concepts on your own.

Word Processing Word-processing software is the most popular computerized productivity tool. In this Lab, you will learn how word-processing software works. When you have completed this Lab, you should be able to apply the general concepts you learned to any word-processing package you use at home, at work, or in your school lab.

1. Click the Steps button to learn how word-processing software works. As you proceed through the Steps, answer all of the Quick Check questions that appear. After you complete the Steps, you will see a Quick Check Summary Report. Follow the instructions on the screen to print this report.

2. Click the Explore button to begin. Click File, then click Open to display the Open dialog box. Click the file **Timber.tex**, then press the Enter key to open the letter to Northern Timber Company. Make the following modifications to the letter, then print it. You do not need to save the letter.

   a. In the first and last lines of the letter, change "Jason Kidder" to your name.
   b. Change the date to today's date.
   c. The second paragraph begins "Your proposal did not include...". Move this paragraph so it is the last paragraph in the text of the letter.
   d. Change the cost of a permanent bridge to $20,000.
   e. Spell check the letter.

3. In Explore, open the file **Stars.tex**. Make the following modifications to the document, then print it. You do not need to save the document.

   a. Center and boldface the title.
   b. Change the title font to size-16 Arial.
   c. Boldface the DATE, SHOWER, and LOCATION.
   d. Move the January 2-3 line to the top of the list.
   e. Double space the entire document.

4. In Explore, compose a one-page double-spaced letter to your parents or to a friend. Make sure you date the letter and check your spelling. Print the letter and sign it. You do not need to save your letter.

INTERNET ASSIGNMENTS

The purpose of the Internet Assignments is to challenge you to find information on the Internet that you can use to create effective documents. The actual assignments are updated and maintained on the Course Technology Web site. Log on to the Internet and use your Web browser to go to the Student Online Companion to accompany this text at **www.course.com/NewPerspectives/office2000**. Click the Word link, and then click the link for Tutorial 1.

QUICK CHECK ANSWERS

Session 1.1

1. (1) Plan the content, purpose, organization, and look of your document. (2) Create and then edit the document. (3) Format the document to make it visually appealing. (4) Preview and then print the document.

2. Click the Start button, point to Programs, and then click Microsoft Word.

3. **a.** symbols you can display on-screen but that don't print

   b. buttons to the left of the horizontal status bar that switch the document to normal view, Web layout view, print layout view, or outline view

   c. actual height of a character measured in points

   d. standard settings

4. Click Format on the menu bar, click Font, select the font size in the Size list box, click the Default button, and then click Yes.

5. Right-click a toolbar, and then click Formatting on the shortcut menu.

6. Click the Normal View button.

Session 1.2

1. Click the Save button on the Standard toolbar, switch to the drive and folder where you want to save the document, enter a filename in the File name text box, and then click the Save button.

2. Anyone can determine the document's purpose without having to open the document and skim it.

3. When you type a word that extends into the right margin, Word moves that word and the insertion point to the next line.

4. An interactive guide to finding information about Word; click the Microsoft Word Help button on the Standard toolbar, type your question and click Search, click the help topic you want to read.

5. **a.** as you type, text shifts out of view

   b. typing dates and other regularly used words and text for you

   c. checks for spelling and grammar errors as you type and fixes common typing errors automatically

   d. shows how the document will look when printed

6. Click the Close button in the upper-right corner of the screen; click File on the menu bar and then click Exit.

In this tutorial you will:

- Open, rename, and save a previously saved document

- Check spelling and grammar

- Move the insertion point around the document

- Select and delete text

- Reverse edits using the Undo and Redo commands

- Move text within the document

- Find and replace text

- Change margins, line spacing, alignment, and paragraph indents

- Copy formatting with the Format Painter

- Emphasize points with bullets, numbering, boldface, underlining, and italics

- Change fonts and adjust font sizes

EDITING AND FORMATTING A DOCUMENT

Preparing an Annuity Plan Description for Right-Hand Solutions

CASE

Right-Hand Solutions

Reginald Thomson is a contract specialist for Right-Hand Solutions, a company that provides small businesses with financial and administrative services. Right-Hand Solutions contracts with independent insurance companies to prepare insurance plans and investment opportunities for these small businesses. Brandi Paxman, vice president of administrative services, asked Reginald to plan and write a document that describes the tax-deferred annuity plan for their clients' employee handbooks. Now that Brandi has commented on and corrected the draft, Reginald asks you to make the necessary changes and print the document.

In this tutorial, you will edit the annuity plan description according to Brandi's comments. You will open a draft of the annuity plan, resave it, and delete a phrase. You will check the plan's grammar and spelling, and then move text using two different methods. Also, you will find and replace one version of the company name with another.

Next, you will change the overall look of the document by changing margins and line spacing, indenting and justifying paragraphs, and copying formatting from one paragraph to another. You'll create a bulleted list to emphasize the types of financial needs the annuity plan will cover and a numbered list for the conditions under which employees can receive funds. Then you'll make the title more prominent by centering it, changing its font, and enlarging it. You'll italicize the questions within the plan to set them off from the rest of the text and underline an added note about how to get further information to give it emphasis. Finally, you will print a copy of the plan.

SESSION 2.1

In In this session you will learn how to use the Spelling and Grammar checker to correct any errors in your document. Then you will edit Reginald's document by deleting words and moving text. Finally, you'll find and replace text throughout the document.

Opening the Document

Brandi's editing marks and notes on the first draft are shown in Figure 2-1. You'll begin by opening the first draft of the description, which has the filename Annuity.

Figure 2-1 **DRAFT OF ANNUITY PLAN SHOWING BRANDI'S EDITS (PAGE 1)**

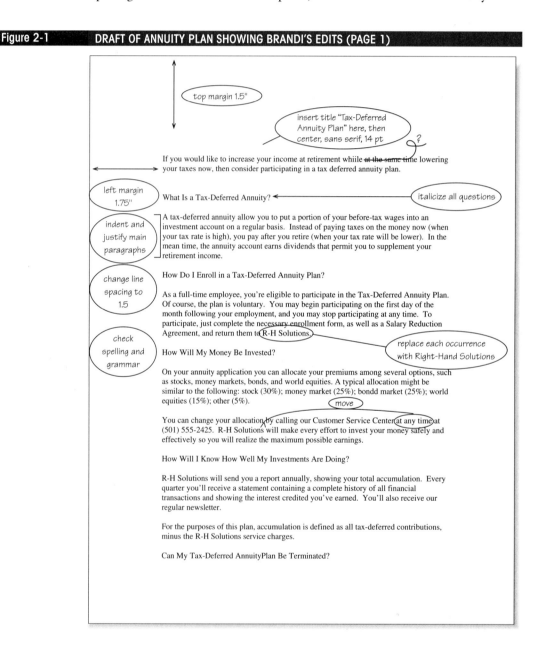

Figure 2-1	DRAFT OF ANNUITY PLAN SHOWING BRANDI'S EDITS (PAGE 2)

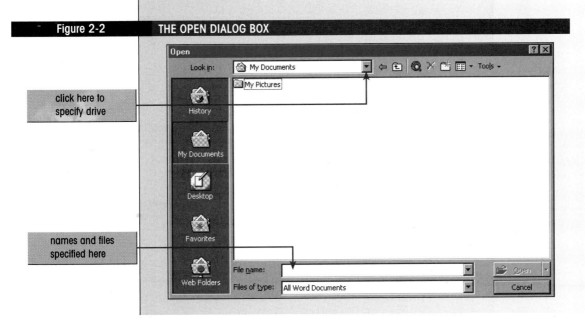

To open the document:

1. Place your Data Disk into the appropriate disk drive.

2. Start Word as usual.

3. Click the **Open** button 📂 on the Standard toolbar to display the Open dialog box, shown in Figure 2-2.

Figure 2-2	THE OPEN DIALOG BOX

4. Click the **Look in** list arrow. The list of drives and files appears.

5. Click the drive that contains your Data Disk.

6. Double-click the **Tutorial.02** folder, then double-click the **Tutorial** folder.

7. Click **Annuity** to select the file, if necessary.

TROUBLE? If you see "Annuity.doc" in the folder, Windows might be configured to display filename extensions. Click Annuity.doc and continue with Step 8. If you can't find the file with or without the filename extension, make sure you're looking in the Tutorial subfolder within the Tutorial.02 folder on the drive that contains your Data Disk, and check to make sure the Files of type text box displays All Word Documents or All Files. If you still can't locate the file, ask your instructor or technical support person for help.

8. Click the **Open** button. The document opens, with the insertion point at the beginning of the document. See Figure 2-3.

Figure 2-3	THE OPEN DOCUMENT

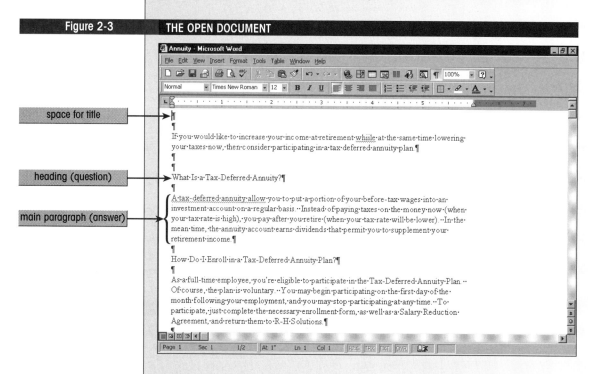

9. Check that your screen matches Figure 2-3. For this tutorial, display the nonprinting characters so that the formatting elements (tabs, paragraph marks, and so forth) are visible and easier to change.

Now that you've opened the document, you can save it with a new name.

Renaming the Document

To avoid altering the original file, Annuity, you will save the document using the filename RHS Annuity Plan. Saving the document with another filename creates a copy of the file and leaves the original file unchanged in case you want to work through the tutorial again.

> ## To save the document with a new name:
>
> 1. Click **File** on the menu bar, and then click **Save As**. The Save As dialog box opens with the current filename highlighted in the File name text box. You could type an entirely new filename, or you could edit the current one. In the next step, practice editing a filename.
>
> 2. Click to the left of "Annuity" in the File name text box, type **RHS**, and then press the **spacebar**. Press the → key to move the insertion point to the right of the letter "y" in "Annuity," press the **spacebar**, and then type **Plan**. The filename changes to RHS Annuity Plan.
>
> 3. Click the **Save** button to save the document with the new filename.

Now you're ready to begin working with the document. First, you will check it for spelling and grammatical errors.

Using the Spelling and Grammar Checker

When typing a document, you can check for spelling and grammatical errors simply by looking for words underlined in red (for spelling errors) or green (for grammatical errors). But when you're working on a document that someone else typed, it's a good idea to start by using the Spelling and Grammar checker. This feature checks a document word by word for a variety of spelling and grammatical errors. Among other things, the Spelling and Grammar checker can sometimes find words that, though spelled correctly, are not used properly. For example, the word "their" instead of the word "there" or "form" instead of "from."

> **REFERENCE WINDOW** RW
>
> ### Checking a Document for Spelling and Grammatical Errors
> - Click at the beginning of the document, then click the Spelling and Grammar button on the Standard toolbar.
> - In the Spelling and Grammar dialog box, review any errors highlighted in color. Grammatical errors appear in green; spelling errors appear in red. Review the possible corrections in the Suggestions list box.
> - To accept a suggested correction, click it in the Suggestions list box. Then click Change to make the correction and continue searching the document for errors.
> - Click Ignore to skip this instance of the highlighted text and continue searching the document for errors.
> - Click Ignore All to skip all instances of the highlighted text and continue searching the document for errors. Click Ignore Rule to skip all instances of a particular grammatical error.
> - To type your correction directly in the document, click outside the Spelling and Grammar dialog box, make the desired correction, and then click Resume in the Spelling and Grammar dialog box.

You'll see how the Spelling and Grammar checker works as you check the annuity plan document for mistakes.

To check the annuity plan document for spelling and grammatical errors:

1. Verify that the insertion point is located at the beginning of the document, to the left of the first paragraph mark.

2. Click the **Spelling and Grammar** button 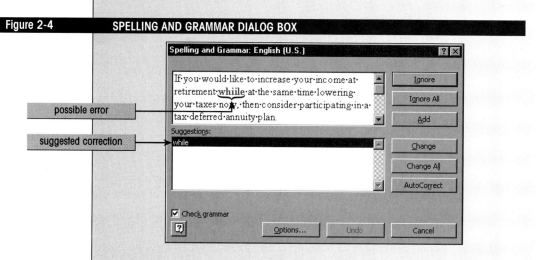 on the Standard toolbar. The Spelling and Grammar dialog box opens with the word "whiile" highlighted in red. The word "while" is suggested as a possible replacement. The line immediately under the title bar indicates the type of problem, in this case, "Not in Dictionary." See Figure 2-4.

| Figure 2-4 | SPELLING AND GRAMMAR DIALOG BOX |

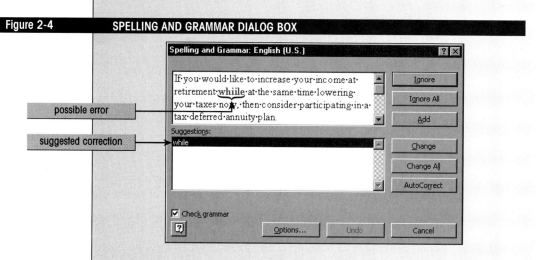

3. Verify that "while" is highlighted in the Suggestions list box, and then click **Change**. "While" is inserted into the document. Next, the grammatical error "A tax-deferred annuity allow" is highlighted in green, with two possible corrections listed in the Suggestions box. The dialog box indicates that the problem concerns subject-verb agreement.

TROUBLE? If you see the word "bondd" selected instead of "a tax-deferred annuity allow," your computer is not set up to check grammar. Click the Check grammar check box to insert a check, and then click Cancel to close the Spelling and Grammar dialog box. Next, click at the beginning of the document, and then repeat Step 2.

4. Click **A tax-deferred annuity allows** in the Suggestions box, if necessary, and then click **Change**. The misspelled word "bondd" is highlighted in red, with two possible replacements listed in the Suggestions list box.

5. Click **bond**, if necessary, to highlight it, and then click **Change**.

6. Click the **Ignore Rule** button to prevent the Spelling and Grammar checker from stopping at each of the remaining seven bullets in the document. You see a message indicating that the spelling and grammar check is complete. The Spelling and Grammar checker next selects the word "tuition," with the capitalized version

> of the same word, "Tuition," listed in the Suggestions box. You do not want to accept the change because the highlighted word is the beginning of a bulleted list, not a sentence, and doesn't have to be capitalized.
>
> **7.** Click **OK**. You return to the annuity plan document.

Although the Spelling and Grammar checker is a useful tool, remember that there is no substitute for careful proofreading. Always take the time to read through your document to check for errors the Spelling and Grammar checker might have missed. Keep in mind that Spelling and Grammar checker probably won't catch *all* instances of words that are spelled correctly but used improperly. And of course, the Spelling and Grammar checker cannot pinpoint phrases that are simply confusing or inaccurate. To produce a professional document, you must read it carefully several times, and, if necessary, ask a co-worker to read it, too.

To proofread the annuity plan document:

1. Scroll to the beginning of the document and begin proofreading.

The first error is a missing hyphen in the phrase "tax deferred annuity plan" at the end of the first paragraph.

2. Click after the "x" in "tax," type – (a hyphen), and then press the **Delete** key to remove the space. Now the phrase is hyphenated correctly.

The next error is the word "mean time" in the paragraph below the "What Is a Tax-Deferred Annuity?" heading. You need to delete the space.

3. Click after the letter "n" in "mean" and then press the **Delete** key.

4. Continue proofreading the document.

Once you are certain the document is free from errors, you are ready to make some more editing changes. To make all of Brandi's editing changes, you'll need to learn how to quickly move the insertion point to any location in the document.

Moving the Insertion Point Around a Document

The arrow keys on your keyboard, ↑, ↓, →, and ←, allow you to move the insertion point one character at a time to the left or right, or one line at a time up or down. If you want to move more than one character or one line at a time, you can point and click in other parts of a line or the document. You also can press a combination of keys to move the insertion point. As you become more experienced with Word, you'll decide which method you prefer.

To see how quickly you can move through the document, you'll use keystrokes to move the insertion point to the beginning of the second page and to the end of the document.

To move the insertion point with keystrokes:

1. Press the **Ctrl** key and hold it down while you press the **Home** key. The insertion point moves to the beginning of the document.

2. Press the **Page Down** key to move the insertion point down to the next screen.

3. Press the **Page Down** key again to move the insertion point down to the next screen.

4. Notice that the status bar indicates the location of the insertion point.

5. Press the ↓ or ↑ key to move the insertion point to the paragraph that begins "Your Tax-deferred Annuity Plan can be terminated...." The insertion point is now at the beginning of page 2. Notice the **automatic page break**, a dotted line that Word inserts automatically to mark the beginning of the new page. See Figure 2-5. As you insert and delete text or change formatting in a document, the location of the automatic page breaks in your document continually adjusts to account for the edits.

Figure 2-5	AUTOMATIC PAGE BREAK

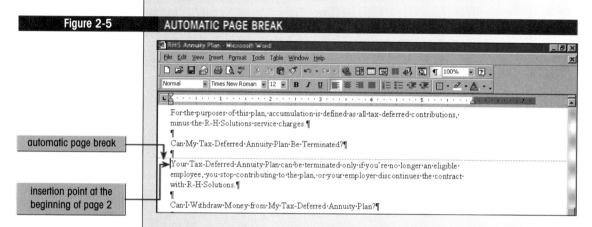

automatic page break

insertion point at the beginning of page 2

6. Press **Ctrl+End**. (That is, press and hold down the **Ctrl** key while you press the **End** key.) The insertion point moves to the end of the document.

7. Use the ← key to move the insertion point immediately before the phrase "at (501) 555-2425," and then type your name and a space.

8. Move the insertion point back to the beginning of the document.

Figure 2-6 summarizes the keystrokes you can use to move the insertion point around the document.

Figure 2-6	KEYSTROKES FOR MOVING THE INSERTION POINT

PRESS	TO MOVE INSERTION POINT
← or →	Left or right one character at a time
↑ or ↓	Up or down one line at a time
Ctrl+← or Ctrl+→	Left or right one word at a time
Ctrl+↑ or Ctrl+↓	Up or down one paragraph at a time
Home or End	To the beginning or to the end of the current line
Ctrl+Home or Ctrl+End	To the beginning or to the end of the document
PageUp or PageDown	To the previous screen or to the next screen
Alt+Ctrl+PageUp or Alt+Ctrl+PageDown	To the top or to the bottom of the document window

Using Select, Then Do

One of the most powerful editing features in Word is the "select, then do" feature. It allows you to select (or highlight) a block of text and then do something to that text, such as deleting, moving, or formatting it. You can select text using either the mouse or the keyboard; however, the mouse is usually the easier and more efficient way. With the mouse, you can quickly select a line or paragraph by clicking the **selection bar**, which is the blank space in the left margin area of the document window. Also, you can select text using various combinations of keys. Figure 2-7 summarizes methods for selecting text with the mouse and the keyboard. The notation "Ctrl+Shift" indicates that you should press and hold two keys (the Ctrl key and the Shift key) at the same time.

Figure 2-7	METHODS FOR SELECTING TEXT WITH THE MOUSE AND KEYBOARD		
TO SELECT	**MOUSE**	**KEYBOARD**	**MOUSE AND KEYBOARD**
A word	Double-click the word.	Move the insertion point to the beginning of the next word, hold down Ctrl+Shift, and then press → once.	
A line	Click in the selection bar next to the line.	Move the insertion point to the beginning of the line, hold down Ctrl+Shift, and then press → until the line is selected.	
A sentence			Press and hold down the Ctrl key, and click within the sentence.
Multiple lines	Click and drag in the selection bar next to the lines.	Move the insertion point to the beginning of the first line, hold down Ctrl+Shift, and then press → until all the lines are selected.	
A paragraph	Double-click in the selection bar next to the paragraph, or triple-click within the paragraph.	Move the insertion point to the beginning of the paragraph, hold down Ctrl+Shift, and then press ↓.	
Multiple paragraphs	Click and drag in the selection bar next to the paragraphs, or triple-click within the first paragraph and drag.	Move the insertion point to the beginning of the first paragraph, hold down Ctrl+Shift, and then press ↓ until all the paragraphs are selected.	
Entire document	Triple-click in the selection bar.	Press Ctrl+A.	Press and hold down the Ctrl key and click in the selection bar.
A block of text			Click at the beginning of the block, press and hold down the Shift key, and then click at the end of the block.

Deleting Text

Brandi wants you to delete the phrase "at the same time" in the first paragraph of the document. You'll use the "select, then do" feature to delete the phrase now.

To select and delete a phrase from the text:

1. Click and drag over the phrase **at the same time** located in the first line of the first paragraph. The phrase and the space following it are highlighted, as shown in Figure 2-8. Notice that dragging the pointer over the second and successive words automatically selects the entire words and the spaces following them. This makes it much easier to select words and phrases than selecting them one character at a time.

Figure 2-8	PHRASE SELECTED FOR DELETION

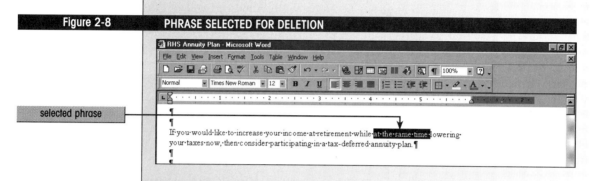

selected phrase

2. Press the **Delete** key. The phrase disappears and the words "lowering your taxes now" move up to the same line as the deleted phrase. See Figure 2-9.

Figure 2-9	PARAGRAPH AFTER DELETING PHRASE

text wrapped back to fill space left by deleted phrase

former location of deleted phrase

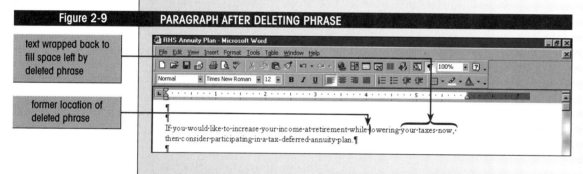

TROUBLE? If your screen looks slightly different than Figure 2-9, don't be concerned. The text may wrap differently on your monitor. Just make sure the phrase has been deleted.

After rereading the paragraph, Reginald decides the phrase shouldn't have been deleted after all. He checks with Brandi, and she agrees. You could retype the text, but there's an easier way to restore the phrase.

Using the Undo and Redo Commands

To undo (or reverse) the very last thing you did, simply click the **Undo button** on the Standard toolbar. If you want to reinstate your original change, the **Redo button** reverses the action of the Undo button (or redoes the undo). To undo anything more than your last action, you can click the Undo list arrow on the Standard toolbar. This list shows your most recent actions. Undo reverses the action only at its original location. You can't delete a word or phrase and then undo it at a different location.

REFERENCE   WINDOW   **RW**

<u>Using Undo and Redo</u>
- Click the Undo button on the Standard toolbar to reverse your last action. Or click Edit on the menu bar, and then click Undo. Note that the exact command you see on the Edit menu will reflect your most recent action, such as "Undo Typing."
- To reverse several previous actions, click the Undo list arrow on the Standard toolbar. Click an action on the list to reverse all actions up to and including the one you click.
- To display a ScreenTip reminder of your last action, place the mouse pointer over the Undo button.
- To undo your previous actions one-by-one, in the reverse order in which you performed them, click the Undo button once for every action you want to reverse.
- If you undo an action by mistake, click the Redo button on the Standard toolbar (or click Edit on the menu bar, and then click Redo) to reverse the undo.

You decide to undo the deletion to see how the sentence reads. Rather than retyping the phrase, you will reverse the edit using the Undo button.

To undo the deletion:

1. Place the mouse pointer over the Undo button ⟲ on the Standard toolbar. The label "Undo Clear" appears in a ScreenTip, indicating that your most recent action involved deleting (or clearing) text.

2. Click the **Undo** button ⟲. The phrase "at the same time" reappears in your document and is highlighted.

   TROUBLE? If the phrase doesn't reappear and something else changes in your document, you probably made another edit or change to the document (such as pressing the Backspace key) between the deletion and the undo. Click the Undo button on the Standard toolbar until the phrase reappears in your document. If a list of possible changes appears under the Undo button, you clicked the list arrow next to the Undo button rather than the Undo button itself. Click the Undo button to restore the deleted phrase and close the list box.

3. Click within the paragraph to deselect the phrase.

   As you read the sentence, you decide that it reads better without the phrase. Instead of deleting it again, you'll redo the undo. As you place the pointer over the Redo button, notice that its ScreenTip indicates the action you want to redo.

4. Place the mouse pointer over the Redo button ⟳ on the Standard toolbar and observe the "Redo Clear" label.

5. Click the **Redo** button ⟳. The phrase "at the same time" disappears from your document again.

6. Click the **Save** button 🖫 on the Standard toolbar to save your changes to the document.

You have edited the document by deleting the text that Brandi marked for deletion. Now, you are ready to make the rest of the edits she suggested.

Moving Text Within a Document

One of the most important uses of "select, then do" is moving text. For example, Brandi wants to reorder the four points Reginald made in the section "Can I Withdraw Money from My Tax-Deferred Annuity Plan?" on page 2 of his draft. You could reorder the list by deleting the sentence and then retyping it at the new location, but a much more efficient approach is to select and then move the sentence. Word provides several ways to move text: drag and drop, cut and paste, and copy and paste.

Dragging and Dropping Text

One way to move text within a document is called drag and drop. With **drag and drop**, you select the text you want to move, press and hold down the mouse button while you drag the selected text to a new location, and then release the mouse button.

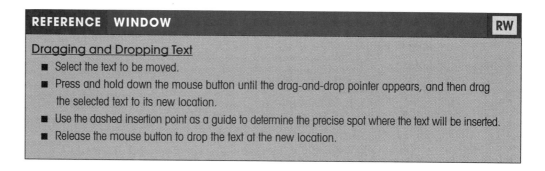

REFERENCE WINDOW **RW**

Dragging and Dropping Text
- Select the text to be moved.
- Press and hold down the mouse button until the drag-and-drop pointer appears, and then drag the selected text to its new location.
- Use the dashed insertion point as a guide to determine the precise spot where the text will be inserted.
- Release the mouse button to drop the text at the new location.

Brandi requested a change in the order of the items in the bulleted list on page 2 of the document, so you'll use the drag-and-drop method to reorder the items. At the same time, you'll practice using the selection bar to highlight a line of text.

To move text using drag and drop:

1. Scroll through the document until you see "tuition for post-secondary education...," the first item in the list of "immediate and severe financial needs:" that begins in the middle of page 2.

2. Click 𝄐 in the selection bar to the left of the line beginning "tuition..." to select that line of text, including the return character. See Figure 2-10.

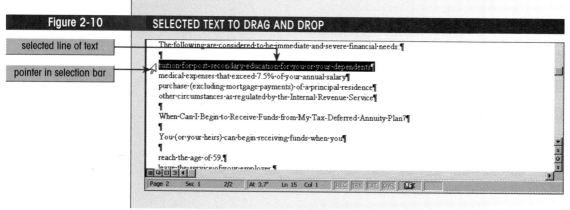

| Figure 2-10 | SELECTED TEXT TO DRAG AND DROP |

selected line of text

pointer in selection bar

The following are considered to be immediate and severe financial needs:¶
¶
tuition for post-secondary education for you or your dependents¶
medical expenses that exceed 7.5% of your annual salary¶
purchase (excluding mortgage payments) of a principal residence¶
other circumstances as regulated by the Internal Revenue Service¶
¶
When Can I Begin to Receive Funds from My Tax-Deferred Annuity Plan?¶
¶
You (or your heirs) can begin receiving funds when you¶
¶
reach the age of 59.¶
leave the service of your employer¶

Page 2   Sec 1   2/2   At 3.7"   Ln 15   Col 1   REC TRK EXT OVR

3. Position the pointer over the selected text. The pointer changes from a right-facing arrow to a left-facing arrow .

4. Press and hold down the mouse button until the drag-and-drop pointer , which has a dashed insertion point, an arrow, and a small square called a move box, appears.

5. Drag the selected text down three lines until the dashed insertion point appears to the left of the word "other." Make sure you use the dashed insertion point to guide the text to its new location rather than the mouse pointer or the move box; the dashed insertion point marks the precise location of the drop. See Figure 2-11.

Figure 2-11	MOVING TEXT WITH DRAG-AND-DROP POINTER

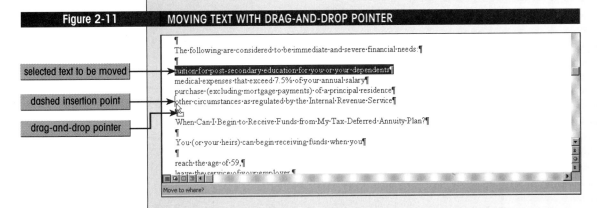

selected text to be moved

dashed insertion point

drag-and-drop pointer

6. Release the mouse button. The selected text moves to its new location, as the third item in the list.

TROUBLE? If the selected text moves to the wrong location, click the Undo button on the Standard toolbar, and then repeat Steps 3 through 6, making sure you hold the mouse button until the dashed insertion point appears in front of the word "other."

7. Deselect the highlighted text by clicking anywhere in the document window.

Dragging and dropping works well if you're moving text a short distance in a document; however, Word provides another method, called cut and paste, that works well for moving text either a short distance or beyond the current screen.

Cutting or Copying and Pasting Text

To **cut** means to remove text from the document and place it on the **Office Clipboard**, which stores up to 12 items at a time. To **paste** means to transfer a copy of the text from the Clipboard into the document at the insertion point. To perform a cut-and-paste action, you select the text you want to move, cut (or remove) it from the document, and then paste (or restore) it into the document in a new location. If you don't want to remove the text from its original location, you can copy it (rather than cutting it) and then paste the copy in a new location. This procedure is known as "copy and paste."

If you cut or copy more than one item, the Clipboard toolbar opens, making it easier for you to select which items you want to paste into the document.

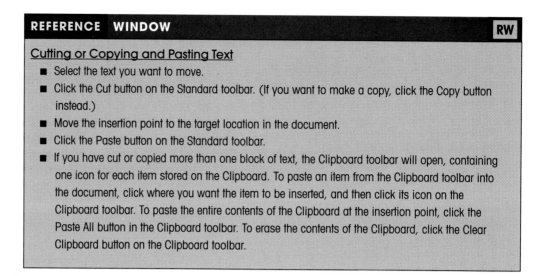

REFERENCE WINDOW   **RW**

<u>Cutting or Copying and Pasting Text</u>
- Select the text you want to move.
- Click the Cut button on the Standard toolbar. (If you want to make a copy, click the Copy button instead.)
- Move the insertion point to the target location in the document.
- Click the Paste button on the Standard toolbar.
- If you have cut or copied more than one block of text, the Clipboard toolbar will open, containing one icon for each item stored on the Clipboard. To paste an item from the Clipboard toolbar into the document, click where you want the item to be inserted, and then click its icon on the Clipboard toolbar. To paste the entire contents of the Clipboard at the insertion point, click the Paste All button in the Clipboard toolbar. To erase the contents of the Clipboard, click the Clear Clipboard button on the Clipboard toolbar.

Brandi suggested moving the phrase "at any time" (in the paragraph beginning "You can change your allocation…") to a new location. You'll use cut and paste to move this phrase.

To move text using cut and paste:

1. Scroll the document up until you can see the paragraph just above the heading "How Will I Know…." on page 1.

2. Click and drag the mouse to highlight the complete phrase **at any time**. See Figure 2-12.

Figure 2-12   **TEXT TO MOVE USING CUT AND PASTE**

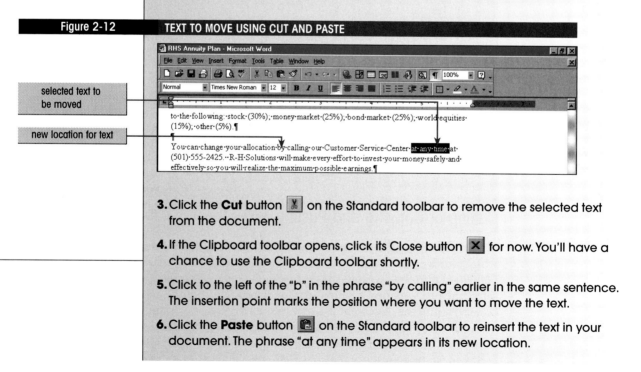

3. Click the **Cut** button on the Standard toolbar to remove the selected text from the document.

4. If the Clipboard toolbar opens, click its Close button for now. You'll have a chance to use the Clipboard toolbar shortly.

5. Click to the left of the "b" in the phrase "by calling" earlier in the same sentence. The insertion point marks the position where you want to move the text.

6. Click the **Paste** button on the Standard toolbar to reinsert the text in your document. The phrase "at any time" appears in its new location.

The copy and paste feature works much the same way as cut and paste. You can try using this technique now, as you copy the phrase "Tax-Deferred Annuity Plan" from the middle of the document and then paste it at the top of the document.

1. Scroll the document up until you can see the heading "How Do I Enroll in a Tax-Deferred Annuity Plan?" on page 1.

2. In the headings, click and drag the mouse to highlight the complete phrase "Tax-Deferred Annuity Plan."

3. Click the **Copy** button 🖹 on the Standard toolbar. The Clipboard toolbar opens, containing icons for each item currently stored on the Clipboard, as shown in Figure 2-13. The "W" on the icons indicates that the copied items contain Word text. Note that your Clipboard toolbar might contain more than two icons, depending on whether you (or another user) cut or copy text before completing this tutorial. You also may see icons for other Office programs, such as Excel.

Figure 2-13	CLIPBOARD TOOLBAR WITH CUT AND COPIED ITEMS

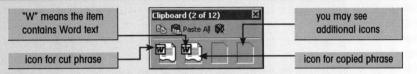

TROUBLE? If the Office Assistant opens, hide it and continue with Step 4.

4. Place the mouse pointer over each of the icons, one at a time, until the ScreenTip "at any time" appears, indicating that this is the icon for the text you cut in the previous set of steps.

5. Place the mouse pointer over each of the icons, one at a time, until the ScreenTip "Tax-Deferred Annuity Plan" appears, indicating that this is the icon for the text you just copied.

6. Scroll up and click at the beginning of the document to move the insertion point there.

7. Click the **Tax-Deferred Annuity Plan** icon in the Clipboard toolbar. The phrase is inserted at the top of the document. Now that you are finished using the Clipboard toolbar, you will delete its contents.

8. Click the **Clear Clipboard** button 🕱 button on the Clipboard toolbar. All of the icons disappear from the Clipboard toolbar.

9. Click the **Close** button ☒ on the Clipboard toolbar. The Clipboard toolbar disappears.

Finding **and Replacing Text**

When you're working with a longer document, the quickest and easiest way to locate a particular word or phrase is to use the Find command. If you want to replace characters or a phrase with something else, you can use the Replace command, which combines the Find command with a substitution feature. The Replace command searches through a document and substitutes the text you're searching for with the replacement text you specify. As Word performs the search, it stops and highlights each occurrence of the search text and lets you determine whether to substitute the replacement text by clicking the Replace button.

If you want to substitute every occurrence of the search text with the replacement text, you can click the Replace All button. When using the Replace All button with single words, keep in mind that the search text might be found within other words. To prevent Word from making incorrect substitutions in such cases, it's a good idea to select the "Find whole words only" check box along with the Replace All button. For example, suppose you want to replace the word "figure" with illustration. Unless you select the "Find whole words only" check box, Word would replace "configure" with "conillustration."

As you search through a document, you can search from the current location of the insertion point down to the end of the document, from the insertion point up to the beginning of the document, or throughout the document.

REFERENCE WINDOW   **RW**

Finding and Replacing Text

- Click the Select Browse Object button on the vertical scroll bar, and then click the Find button on the Select Browse Object menu. (You also can click Edit on the menu bar, and then click either Find or Replace.)
- To find text, click the Find tab; or, to find and replace text, click the Replace tab.
- Click the More button to expand the dialog box to display additional options (including the "Find whole words only" option). If you see the Less button, the additional options are already displayed.
- In the Search list box, select Down if you want to search from the insertion point to the end of the document, select Up if you want to search from the insertion point to the beginning of the document, or select All to search the entire document.
- Type the characters you want to find in the Find what text box.
- If you are replacing text, type the replacement text in the Replace with text box.
- Click the Find Next button.
- Click the Replace button to substitute the found text with the replacement text and find the next occurrence.
- Click the Find whole words only check box, and then click the Replace All button to substitute all occurrences of the found text with the replacement text.

Brandi wants the shortened version of the company name, "R-H Solutions," to be spelled out as "Right-Hand Solutions" every time it appears in the text.

To replace "R-H Solutions" with "Right-Hand Solutions:"

1. Click the **Select Browse Object** button ⊙ near the bottom of the vertical scroll bar.

2. Click the **Find** button 🔍 on the Select Browse Object menu. The Find and Replace dialog box appears.

3. Click the **Replace** tab.

4. If necessary, click the **More** button to display the additional search options.

5. If necessary, click the **Search** list arrow, and then click **All**.

6. Click the **Find what** text box, type **R-H Solutions**, press the **Tab** key, and then type **Right-Hand Solutions** in the Replace with text box. Note that because the search text is made up of more than one word, the "Find whole words only" option is unnecessary and is therefore unavailable. See Figure 2-14.

Figure 2-14	FIND AND REPLACE DIALOG BOX

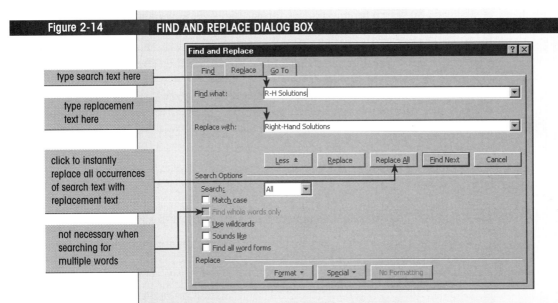

type search text here

type replacement text here

click to instantly replace all occurrences of search text with replacement text

not necessary when searching for multiple words

TROUBLE? If you already see the text "R-H Solutions" and "Right-Hand Solutions" in your Find and Replace dialog box, someone already performed these steps on your computer. Simply continue with Step 7.

7. Click the **Replace All** button to replace all occurrences of the search text with the replacement text. When Word finishes making the replacements, you see a dialog box telling you that six replacements were made.

8. Click **OK** to close the dialog box, and then click the **Close** button in the Find and Replace dialog box to return to the document. The full company name has been inserted into the document, as shown in Figure 2-15.

Figure 2-15	THE NAME "RIGHT-HAND SOLUTIONS" INSERTED INTO THE DOCUMENT

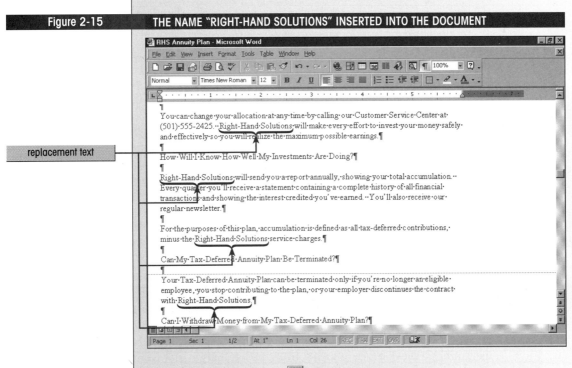

replacement text

9. Click the **Save** button 🖫 on the Standard toolbar to save your changes to the document.

You can also search for and replace formatting, such as bold, and special characters, such as paragraph marks, in the Find and Replace dialog box. Click in the Find what text box or the Replace with text box, enter any text if necessary, click the Format button, click Font to open the Font dialog box, and then select the formatting you want to find or replace. Complete the search or replace as usual.

You have completed the content changes Brandi suggested, but she has some other changes that will improve the plan's appearance. In the next session, you'll enhance the annuity plan by changing the width, spacing, and alignment of text.

Session 2.1 QUICK CHECK

1. Explain how to open a document and save a copy of it with a new name.

2. Which key(s) do you press to move the insertion point to the following places:

   a. down one line
   b. end of the document
   c. to the next screen

3. Describe the "select, then do" feature.

4. Define the following terms in your own words:

   a. selection bar
   b. Redo button
   c. drag and drop

5. Explain how to select a single word. Explain how to select a complete paragraph.

6. Describe a situation in which you would use the Undo button and then the Redo button.

7. True or False: You can use the Redo command to restore deleted text at a new location in your document.

8. What is the difference between cut and paste, and copy and paste?

9. List the steps involved in finding and replacing text in a document.

SESSION 2.2

In this session you will make the formatting changes Brandi suggested. You'll use a variety of formatting commands to change the margins, line spacing, text alignment, and paragraph indents. Also, you'll learn how to use the Format Painter, how to create bulleted and numbered lists, and how to change fonts, font sizes, and emphasis.

Changing the Margins

In general, it's best to begin formatting by making the changes that affect the document's overall appearance. Then you can make changes that affect only selected text. In this case, you need to adjust the margin settings of the annuity plan summary.

Word uses default margins of 1.25 inches for the left and right margins and 1 inch for the top and bottom margins. The numbers on the ruler (displayed below the Formatting toolbar) indicate the distance in inches from the left margin, not from the left edge of the paper. Unless you specify otherwise, changes you make to the margins will affect the entire document, not just the current paragraph or page.

REFERENCE   WINDOW   **RW**

Changing Margins for the Entire Document
- With the insertion point anywhere in your document and no text selected, click File on the menu bar, and then click Page Setup.
- If necessary, click the Margins tab to display the margin settings.
- Use the arrows to change the settings in the Top, Bottom, Left, or Right text boxes, or type a new margin value in each text box.
- Make sure the Apply to list box displays Whole document.
- Click the OK button.

You need to change the top margin to 1.5 inches and the left margin to 1.75 inches, as Brandi requested. The left margin needs to be wider than usual to allow space for making holes so that the document can be inserted in a three-ring binder. In the next set of steps, you'll change the margins with the Page Setup command. You also can change margins in print layout view; you'll practice that method in the Review Assignments.

To change the margins in the annuity plan document:

1. If you took a break after the last lesson, make sure Word is running, the RHS Annuity Plan document is open, and nonprinting characters are displayed.

2. Click once anywhere in the document to make sure no text is selected.

3. Click **File** on the menu bar, and then click **Page Setup** to open the Page Setup dialog box.

4. If necessary, click the **Margins** tab to display the margin settings. The Top margin setting is selected. See Figure 2-16.

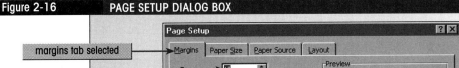

Figure 2-16   PAGE SETUP DIALOG BOX

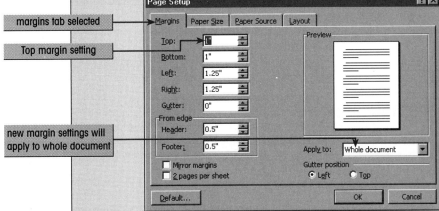

margins tab selected

Top margin setting

new margin settings will apply to whole document

5. Type **1.5** to change the Top margin setting. (You do not have to type the inches symbol.)

6. Press the **Tab** key twice to move to the Left text box and select the current margin setting. Notice how the text area in the Preview box moves down to reflect the larger top margin.

7. Type **1.75** and then press the **Tab** key. Watch the Preview box to see how the margin increases.

8. Make sure the **Whole document** option is selected in the Apply to list box, and then click the **OK** button to return to your document. Notice that the right margin on the ruler has changed to reflect the larger margins and the reduced page area that results. See Figure 2-17.

Figure 2-17 | **RULER AFTER SETTING LEFT MARGIN TO 1.75 INCHES**

ruler

text width now 5.5 inches

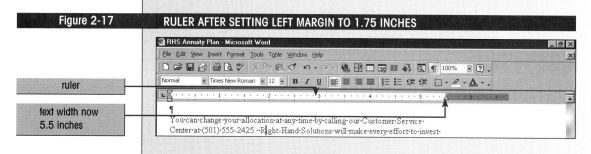

TROUBLE? If a double dotted line and the words "Section Break" appear in your document, text was selected in the document and Whole document wasn't specified in the Apply to list box. If this occurs, click the Undo button on the Standard toolbar and then repeat Steps 1 through 8, making sure you select the Whole document option in the Apply to list box.

Now that you've made numerous changes to your document, it's a good idea to save it with a new name. That way, if the file you are working on somehow becomes corrupted, you can at least return to the earlier draft, rather than having to start all over again.

To save the document with a new name:

1. Click **File** on the menu bar, then click **Save As**.

2. Verify that the Tutorial subfolder within the Tutorial.02 folder appears in the Save in list box, change the filename to **RHS Annuity Plan Copy 2**, and then click the **Save** button. The document is saved with the new margin settings and a new name.

Next you will change the amount of space between lines of text.

Changing Line Spacing

The line spacing in a document determines the amount of vertical space between lines of text. You have a choice of three basic types of line spacing: **single spacing** (which allows for the largest character in a particular line as well as a small amount of extra space); **1.5 line spacing** (which allows for one and one-half times the space of single spacing); and **double spacing** (which allows for twice the space of single spacing). The annuity plan document is currently single-spaced because Word uses single spacing by default. Before changing the line-spacing setting, you should select the text you want to change. You can change line spacing by using the Paragraph command on the Format menu, or by using your keyboard.

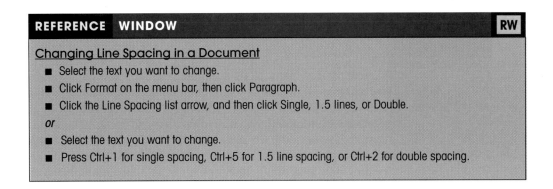

REFERENCE WINDOW RW

Changing Line Spacing in a Document
- Select the text you want to change.
- Click Format on the menu bar, then click Paragraph.
- Click the Line Spacing list arrow, and then click Single, 1.5 lines, or Double.

or

- Select the text you want to change.
- Press Ctrl+1 for single spacing, Ctrl+5 for 1.5 line spacing, or Ctrl+2 for double spacing.

Brandi has asked you to change the line spacing for the entire annuity plan document to 1.5 line spacing. You will begin by selecting the entire document.

To change the document's line spacing:

1. Triple-click in the selection bar to select the entire document.

2. Click **Format** on the menu bar, and then click **Paragraph** to open the Paragraph dialog box.

3. If necessary, click the **Indents and Spacing** tab.

4. Click the **Line spacing** list arrow, and then click **1.5 lines**. The Preview box shows the results of the new line spacing. See Figure 2-18.

| Figure 2-18 | CHANGING THE DOCUMENT'S LINE SPACING |

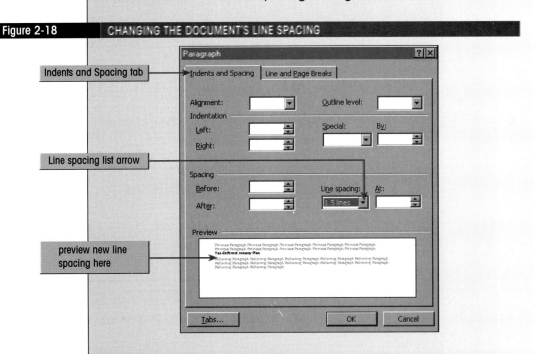

5. Click the **OK** button, and then click anywhere in the document to deselect it. Notice the additional space between every line of text in the document.

Now, you are ready to make formatting changes that affect individual paragraphs.

Aligning Text

Word defines a **paragraph** as any text that ends with a paragraph mark symbol (¶). The alignment of a paragraph or document refers to how the text lines up horizontally between the margins. By default, text is aligned along the left margin but is **ragged**, or uneven, along the right margin. This is called **left alignment**. With **right alignment**, the text is aligned along the right margin and is ragged along the left margin. With **center alignment**, text is centered between the left and right margins. With **justified alignment**, full lines of text are spaced between or aligned along both the left and the right margins. The paragraph you are reading now is justified. The easiest way to apply alignment settings is by clicking buttons on the Formatting toolbar.

Brandi indicated that the title of the annuity plan description should be centered and that the main paragraphs should be justified. First, you'll center the title.

To center-align the title:

1. Click anywhere in the title "Tax-Deferred Annuity Plan" at the beginning of the document.

2. Click the **Center** button on the Formatting toolbar. The text centers between the left and right margins. See Figure 2-19.

| Figure 2-19 | TITLE CENTERED |

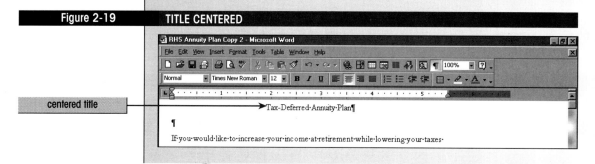

centered title

Now, you'll justify the text in the first two main paragraphs.

To justify the first two paragraphs using the Formatting toolbar:

1. Click anywhere in the first paragraph, which begins "If you would like to increase...," and click the **Justify** button on the Formatting toolbar. The justification would be easier to see if the paragraph had more lines of text. You'll see the effects more clearly after you justify the second paragraph in the document.

2. Move the insertion point to the second main paragraph, which begins "A tax-deferred annuity allows... ."

3. Click again. The text is evenly spaced between the left and right margins. See Figure 2-20.

Figure 2-20	TEXT JUSTIFIED USING THE FORMATTING TOOLBAR

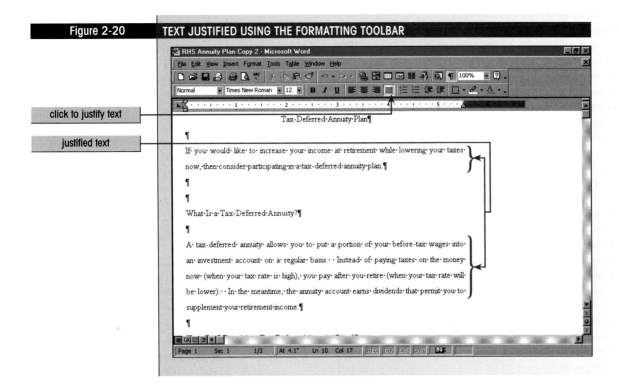

click to justify text

justified text

You'll justify the other paragraphs later. Now that you've learned how to change the paragraph alignment, you can turn your attention to indenting a paragraph.

Indenting a Paragraph

When you become a more experienced Word user, you might want to use some special forms of paragraph formatting, such as a **hanging indent** (where all lines except the first line of the paragraph are indented from the left margin) or a **right indent** (where all lines of the paragraph are indented from the right margin). You can select these types of indents on the Indents and Spacing tab of the Paragraph dialog box.

In this document, though, you'll need to indent only the main paragraphs 0.5 inches from the left margin. This left indent is a simple kind of paragraph indent, which requires only a quick click on the Formatting toolbar's Increase Indent button. According to Brandi's notes, you need to indent all of the main paragraphs, starting with the second paragraph.

To indent a paragraph using the Increase Indent button:

1. Make sure the insertion point is still located anywhere within the second paragraph, which begins "A tax-deferred annuity allows... ."

2. Click the **Increase Indent** button ⊞ on the Formatting toolbar twice. (Don't click the Decrease Indent button by mistake.) The entire paragraph moves right 0.5 inches each time you click the Increase Indent button. The paragraph is indented 1 inch, 0.5 inches more than Brandi wants.

3. Click the **Decrease Indent** button ⊞ on the Formatting toolbar to move the paragraph left 0.5 inches. The paragraph is now indented 0.5 inches from the left margin, as shown in Figure 2-21.

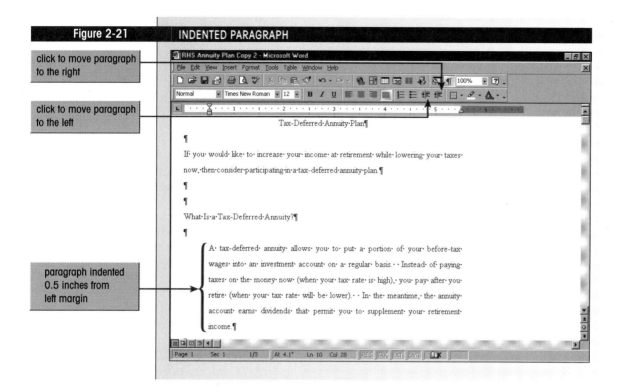

Figure 2-21   INDENTED PARAGRAPH

click to move paragraph to the right

click to move paragraph to the left

paragraph indented 0.5 inches from left margin

You could continue to indent, and then justify, each paragraph individually, but there's an easier way—the Format Painter command. The Format Painter allows you to copy both the indentation and alignment changes to all the other main paragraphs in the document.

Using Format Painter

The **Format Painter** makes it easy to copy all the formatting features of one paragraph to one or more other paragraphs. You'll use the Format Painter now to copy the formatting of the second paragraph to other main paragraphs. Begin by highlighting the paragraph whose format you want to copy. (Note that you can't simply move the insertion point to that paragraph.)

To copy paragraph formatting with the Format Painter:

1. Double-click in the selection bar to select the second paragraph, which is indented and justified and begins "A tax-deferred annuity... ."

2. Double-click the **Format Painter** button 🖌 on the Standard toolbar. The Format Painter button will stay pressed until you click the button again. When you move the pointer over text, the pointer changes to 🖌I to indicate that the format of the selected paragraph can be painted (or copied) onto another paragraph.

3. Scroll down, and then click anywhere in the third paragraph, which begins "As a full-time employee... ." The format of the third paragraph shifts to match the format of the selected paragraph. See Figure 2-22. As you can see, both paragraphs are now indented and justified. The pointer remains as the Format Painter pointer.

Figure 2-22	FORMATS COPIED WITH FORMAT PAINTER

active Format Painter button

paragraph with new formatting

wages· into· an· investment· account· on· a· regular· basis. · · Instead· of· paying·
taxes· on· the· money· now· (when· your· tax· rate· is· high), · you· pay· after· you·
retire· (when· your· tax· rate· will· be· lower). · · In· the· meantime, · the· annuity·
account· earns· dividends· that· permit· you· to· supplement· your· retirement·
income. ¶

¶

How·Do·I·Enroll·in·a·Tax-Deferred·Annuity·Plan? ¶

¶

Format Painter pointer

As· a· full-time· employee, · you're· eligible· to· participate· in· the· Tax-Deferred·
Annuity· Plan· · · Of· course, · the· plan· is· voluntary. · · You· may· begin·
participating· on· the· first· day· of· the· month· following· your· employment, · and·
you· may· stop· participating· at· any· time. · · To· participate, · just· complete· the·
necessary· enrollment· form, · as· well· as· a· Salary· Reduction· Agreement, · and·
return·them·to·Right-Hand·Solutions. ¶

Use the mouse to apply the previously copied paragraph formatting onto other text, or press Esc to cancel.

4. Click each of the remaining paragraphs in the document, one by one, to align and indent them the same way as the second paragraph. Be sure to indent the two lists and any one-line paragraphs that are *not* questions. Do not click the document title, the first paragraph in the document, or one-line questions.

TROUBLE? If you click a paragraph and the formatting doesn't change to match the second paragraph, you single-clicked the Format Painter button rather than double-clicking it. Select a paragraph that has the desired format, double-click the Format Painter button, and then repeat Step 4.

TROUBLE? If you accidentally click a title or one line of a list, click the Undo button on the Standard toolbar to return the line to its original formatting. Then select a paragraph that has the desired format, double-click the Format Painter button, and finish copying the format to the main paragraphs in the document.

5. After you've formatted all the main paragraphs with the Format Painter, click [icon] to turn off the feature.

6. Click the **Save** button [icon] on the Standard toolbar.

All the main paragraphs in the document are formatted with the correct indentation and alignment. Your next job is to make the lists easier to read by adding bullets and numbers.

Adding Bullets and Numbers

You can emphasize a list of items by adding a heavy dot, known as a **bullet**, before each item in the list. For consecutive items, you can use numbers instead of bullets. Brandi requested that you add bullets to the list of financial needs on page 3 to make them stand out.

To apply bullets to a list of items:

1. Scroll the document until you see the list of financial needs below the sentence "The following are considered to be immediate and severe financial needs."

2. Select the four items that appear in the middle of page 3 (from "medical expenses" to "Internal Revenue Service").

3. Click the **Bullets** button on the Formatting toolbar to activate the Bullets feature. A rounded bullet, a special character, appears in front of each item, and each line indents to make room for the bullet.

4. Click anywhere within the document window to deselect the text. Figure 2-23 shows the indented bulleted list.

Figure 2-23   INDENTED BULLETED LIST

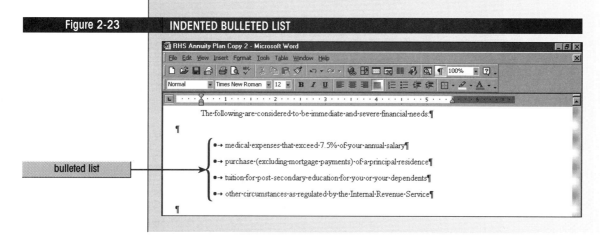

bulleted list

Next you need to add numbers to the list that explains when benefits can be received, in the section below the bulleted list. For this, you'll use the Numbering button, which automatically numbers the selected paragraphs with consecutive numbers and aligns them. If you insert a new paragraph, delete a paragraph, or reorder the paragraphs, Word automatically adjusts the numbers to make sure they remain consecutive.

To apply numbers to the list of items:

1. Scroll down to the next section, and then select the list that begins "reach the age..." and ends with "...become disabled."

2. Click the **Numbering** button on the Formatting toolbar. Consecutive numbers appear in front of each item in the indented list. The list is indented, similar to the bulleted list above.

3. Click anywhere in the document to deselect the text. Figure 2-24 shows the indented and numbered list.

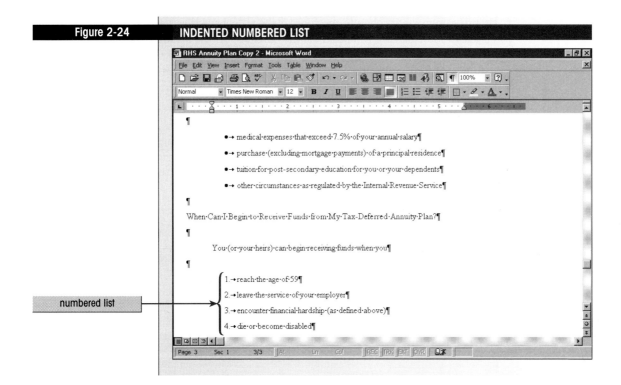

Figure 2-24 INDENTED NUMBERED LIST

The text of the document is now properly aligned and indented. The bullets and numbers make the lists easy to read and give readers visual clues about the type of information they contain. Next, you need to adjust the formatting of individual words.

Changing the Font and Font Size

All of Brandi's remaining changes concern changing fonts, adjusting font sizes, and emphasizing text with font styles. The first step is to change the font of the title from 12-point Times New Roman to 14-point Arial. This will make the title stand out from the rest of the text.

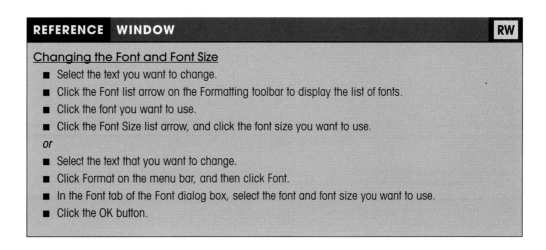

REFERENCE WINDOW RW

Changing the Font and Font Size
- Select the text you want to change.
- Click the Font list arrow on the Formatting toolbar to display the list of fonts.
- Click the font you want to use.
- Click the Font Size list arrow, and click the font size you want to use.

or
- Select the text that you want to change.
- Click Format on the menu bar, and then click Font.
- In the Font tab of the Font dialog box, select the font and font size you want to use.
- Click the OK button.

Brandi wants you to change the font of the title as well as its size and style. To do this, you'll use the Formatting toolbar. Brandi wants you to use a **sans serif** font, which is a font that does not have the small horizontal lines (called serifs) at the tops and bottoms of the letters. Sans serif fonts are often used in titles so they contrast with the body text. Times New Roman is a serif font, and Arial is a sans serif font. The text you are reading now is a serif font, and the text in the steps below is a sans serif font.

To change the attributes of the title using the Font command:

1. Press **Ctrl+Home** to move to the beginning of the document, and then select the title.

2. Click the **Font** list arrow on the Formatting toolbar. A list of available fonts appears in alphabetical order, with the name of the current font highlighted in the font list and in the Font text box. See Figure 2-25. (Your list of fonts might be different from those shown.) Fonts that have been used recently might appear above a double line. Note that each name in the list is formatted with that font. For example, "Arial" appears in the Arial font, and "Times New Roman" appears in the Times New Roman font.

Figure 2-25	FONT LIST

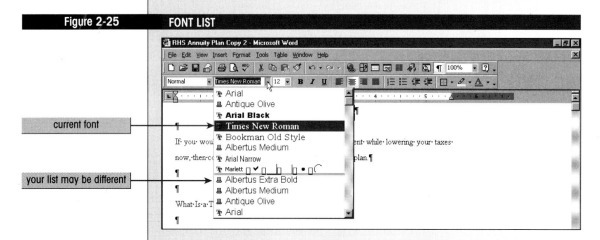

3. If necessary, scroll the list box until Arial appears, and then click **Arial** to select it as the new font. As you click, watch the font in the title change to reflect the new font.

   TROUBLE? If Arial doesn't appear in the font list, use another sans serif font.

4. Click the **Font Size** list arrow on the Formatting toolbar, and then click **14** in the size list. As you click, watch the title's font increase from 12 to 14 point.

5. Click the **Save** button 🖫 on the Standard toolbar to save your changes, and then click within the title to deselect it. See Figure 2-26.

Figure 2-26	TITLE FONT AND FONT SIZE CHANGED

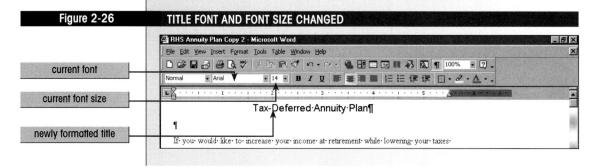

TROUBLE? If your font and font size settings don't match those in Figure 2-26, you may not have selected the title. Select the title, view the font and font size settings displayed on the Formatting toolbar, and then make the necessary changes. Because of differences in fonts and monitors, the characters in your document might look different from the figure.

Emphasizing Text with Boldface, Underlining, and Italics

You can emphasize words in your document with boldface, underlining, or italics. These styles help you make specific thoughts, ideas, words, or phrases stand out. Brandi marked a few words on the document draft (shown in Figure 2-1) that need this kind of special emphasis. You add boldface, underlining, or italics by using the relevant buttons on the Formatting toolbar. Note that these buttons are toggle buttons, which means you can click them once to format the selected text, and then click again to remove the formatting from the selected text.

Bolding Text

Brandi wants to make sure that clients' employees see that the tax-deferred annuity plan can be terminated only under certain conditions. You will do this by bolding the word "only."

To change the font style to boldface:

1. Scroll down so you can view the first line of the paragraph beneath the question "Can My Tax-Deferred Annuity Plan Be Terminated?" on page 2.

2. Select the word "only" (immediately after the word "terminated").

3. Click the **Bold** button B on the Formatting toolbar, and then click anywhere in the document to deselect the text. The word appears in bold, as shown in Figure 2-27. After reviewing this change, you wonder if the word would look better without boldface. As you will see in the next step, you can easily remove the boldface by selecting the text and clicking the Bold button again to turn off boldfacing.

Figure 2-27	WORD IN BOLDFACE

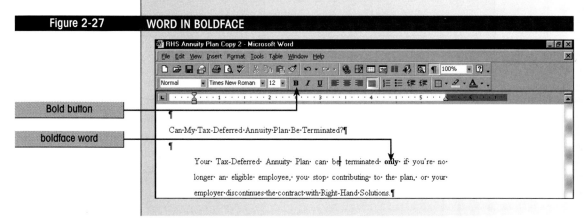

4. Double-click the word **only** to select it, then click 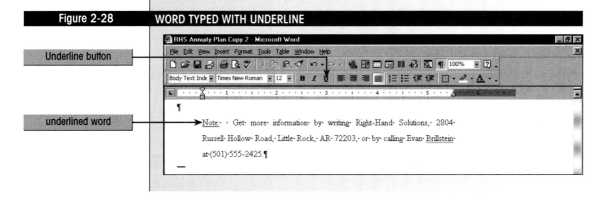**B**. The word now appears without boldface. You decide you prefer to emphasize the word with boldface after all.

5. Verify that the word "only" is still selected, and then click **B**. The word appears in boldface again.

Underlining Text

The Underline command works in the same way as the Bold command. Brandi's edits indicate that the word "Note" should be inserted and underlined at the beginning of the final paragraph. You'll make both of these changes at once using the Underline command.

To underline text:

1. Press **Ctrl+End** to move the insertion point to the end of the document. Then move the insertion point to the left of the word "Get" in the first line of the final paragraph.

2. Click the **Underline** button **U** on the Formatting toolbar to turn on underlining. Notice that the Underline button remains pressed. Now, whatever text you type will be underlined on your screen and in your printed document.

3. Type **Note:** and then click **U** to turn off underlining. Notice that the Underline button is no longer pressed, and "Note:" is underlined.

4. Press the **spacebar** twice. See Figure 2-28.

Figure 2-28	WORD TYPED WITH UNDERLINE

Underline button

underlined word

Note: · Get· more· information· by· writing· Right-Hand· Solutions,· 2804·
Russell· Hollow· Road,· Little· Rock,· AR· 72203,· or· by· calling· Evan· Brillstein·
at·(501)·555-2425.¶

Italicizing Text

Next, you'll make the annuity plan conform with the other documents that Right-Hand Solutions produces by changing each question (heading) in the document to italics. This makes the document easier to read by clearly separating the sections. You'll begin with the first heading.

To italicize the question headings:

1. Press **Ctrl+Home** to return to the beginning of the document, and then select the text of the first heading, "What Is a Tax-Deferred Annuity?," by triple-clicking the text.

2. Click the **Italic** button [I] on the Formatting toolbar. The heading changes from regular to italic text.

3. Repeat Steps 1 and 2 to italicize the next heading. Now try a shorter way to italicize the text by repeating the formatting you just applied.

4. Select the next heading, and then press the **F4** key. Repeat for each of the remaining four questions (headings) in the document. The italicized headings stand out from the rest of the text and help give the document a visual structure.

Saving and Printing

You have made all the editing and formatting changes that Brandi requested for the annuity plan description. When a document is complete, it's a good idea to save it with a name that indicates that it is final. After saving the document, you can preview and print it. It's especially useful to preview a document before printing when you made a number of formatting changes because the Print Preview window makes it easy to spot text that is not aligned correctly.

To save, preview, and print the document:

1. Click **File** on the menu bar, and then click **Save As**. Save the file as **RHS Annuity Plan Final Copy** in the Tutorial subfolder, within the Tutorial.02 folder.

2. Move the insertion point to the beginning of the document.

3. Click the **Print Preview** button [🔍] on the Standard toolbar, and examine the first page of the document. Use the vertical scroll bar to display the second and third pages. (If you notice any headings as the last line of a page or other formatting errors, click the Close button on the Print Preview toolbar, correct the errors in normal view, and then return to the Print Preview window. To move a heading to the next page with its paragraph, click at the beginning of the heading and press **Ctrl+Enter** to insert a manual page break.)

4. Click the **Print** button [🖨] on the Print Preview toolbar. After a pause, the document prints.

5. Click the **Close** button on the Print Preview toolbar, and then click the **Close** button [X] on the program window to close your document and exit Word.

You now have a hardcopy of the final annuity plan description, as shown in Figure 2-29.

Figure 2-29 FINAL VERSION OF RHS ANNUITY PLAN

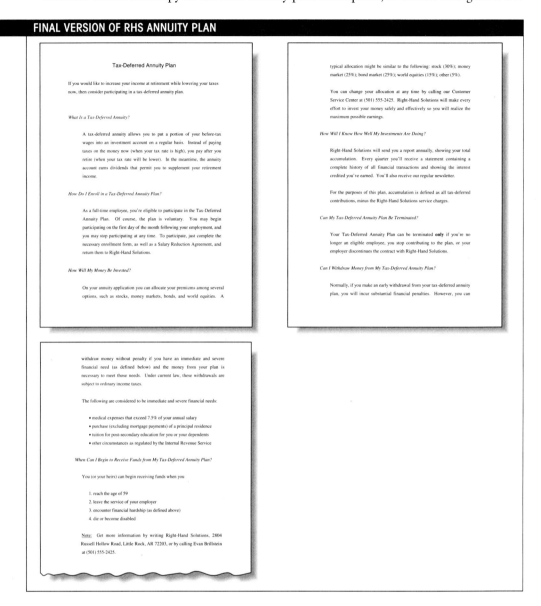

In this tutorial, you have helped Reginald plan, edit, and format the annuity plan that will appear in the employee handbooks of Right-Hand Solutions' clients. Now that you have fine-tuned the content, adjusted the text appearance and alignment, and added a bulleted list and a numbered list, the plan is visually appealing and easy to read.

You give the hardcopy to Reginald, who makes two photocopies—one for Brandi and one for the copy center, which copies and distributes the document to all clients of Right-Hand Solutions.

Session 2.2 QUICK CHECK

1. What are Word's default margins for the left and right margins? For the top and bottom margins?
2. Describe the four types of text alignment.
3. Explain how to indent a paragraph 1 inch or more from the left margin.
4. Describe a situation in which you would use the Format Painter.
5. Explain how to add underlining to a word as you type it.
6. Explain how to transform a series of short paragraphs into a numbered list.

7. Explain how to format a title in 14-point Arial.

8. Describe the steps involved in changing the line spacing in a document.

REVIEW ASSIGNMENTS

Now that you have completed the description of the annuity plan, Brandi explains that she also wants to include a sample quarterly statement and a sample contract change notice in the client's employee handbooks to show employees how easy the statements are to read. You'll open and format this document now.

1. If necessary, start Word, make sure your Data Disk is in the appropriate disk drive, and check your screen to make sure your settings match those in the tutorial.

2. Open the file **RHSQuart** from the Review folder for Tutorial 2 on your Data Disk, and save the document as **RHS Quarterly Report**.

3. Use the Spelling and Grammar checker to correct any spelling or grammatical errors. If the Suggestions list box does not include the correct replacement, click outside the Spelling and Grammar dialog box, type the correction yourself, click Resume in the Spelling and Grammar dialog box, and continue checking the document. After you finish using the Spelling and Grammar checker, proofread the document carefully to check for any additional errors, especially words that are spelled correctly but used improperly. Pay special attention to the second main paragraph of the letter.

4. Make all edits and formatting changes marked on Figure 2-30. To substitute "Right-Hand Solutions" for "We" in the first paragraph, copy the company name from the top of the letter (without the paragraph mark) and paste it into the first paragraph as marked. (Copy and paste this text *before* you format it in Arial 14 point.)

Figure 2-30

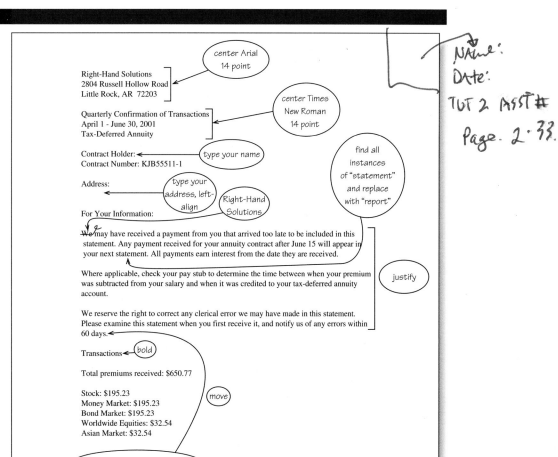

5. Save the document, preview it, and then print it.

6. Close th document.

7. Open the file **RHSPort** from the Review folder for Tutorial 2 on your Data Disk, and save the file as **RHS Portfolio Changes**.

Explore

8. Make all the edits and formatting changes marked on Figure 2-31. However, instead of using the Formatting toolbar to change Current Allocation Accounts to underline 14 point, click Format on the menu bar, and then click Font to open the Font dialog box. Click the appropriate selections in the Underline style and Size list boxes. Notice that you should only replace "Right-Hand Solutions" with "RHS" in the list of Allocation Accounts. To skip an instance of "Right-Hand Solutions" without changing it, click the Find Next button in the Find and Replace dialog box.

Figure 2-31

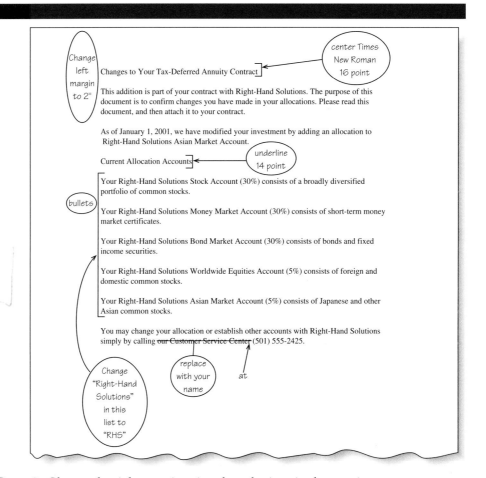

Explore

9. Change the right margin using the ruler in print layout view:
   a. Click the Print Layout View button, and then select the entire document.
   b. Position the pointer on the ruler at the right margin, above the Right Indent marker (a small, gray triangle).
   c. Press and hold down the mouse button. A dotted line appears in the document window, indicating the current right margin. Drag the margin left to the 5-inch mark on the ruler, and then release the mouse button.
   d. Click the Normal View button to return to normal view.
   e. Save the document.

Explore

10. Change the line spacing of individual paragraphs within the document.
   a. Select the first two paragraphs in the document, immediately under the heading "Changes to Your Tax-Deferred Annuity Contract."
   b. Press Ctrl+5 to change the line spacing of the selected paragraphs to 1.5 line spacing.
   c. Save the document.

1. TUT 2 ASST 5 Quickstone
2. TUT 2 13
3. " " CP 1
4. " " CP 2
Due tuesday 26th

11. Cut and paste text using the Clipboard:
    a. Select the second sentence in the document ("The purpose of this document is to confirm…"), and then click the Cut button on the Standard toolbar to remove the sentence from the document. If the Clipboard toolbar appears, leave it open while you continue with the next step.
    b. Select the last sentence in the document ("You may change your allocation…"), and then click the Cut button on the Standard toolbar to remove the sentence from the document. If the Clipboard toolbar did not open at the end of the previous step, it should be open now.
    c. Move the insertion point to the beginning of the first sentence, to the left of the "T" in "This addition is part of your contract… ." Move the pointer over the icons on the Clipboard toolbar, until you find one labeled "The purpose of this document is to confirm… ." Click that icon to insert the sentence (which was originally the second sentence in the document) at the insertion point. Insert an extra space, if necessary.
    d. Repeat the previous step to insert the sentence beginning, "You may change your allocation or establish other…" at the end of the second paragraph.
    e. Click the Clear Clipboard button on the Clipboard toolbar to erase the contents of the Clipboard, and then click the Close button to close the Clipboard toolbar.
12. Click the Print Preview button on the Standard toolbar to check your work.

Explore

13. Use the Print command on the File menu to open the Print dialog box. Print two copies of the document by changing the Number of copies setting in the Print dialog box.

Explore

14. You can find out the number of words in your documents by using the Word Count command on the Tools menu. Use this command to determine the number of words in the document, and then write that number in the upper-right corner of one of the printouts.
15. Save and close the document.

CASE PROBLEMS

Case 1. Store-It-All Katie Strainchamps manages Store-It-All, a storage facility in Huntsville, Alabama. She has written the draft of a tenant-information sheet outlining Store-It-All's policies for new customers. She asks you to edit and format the document for her.

1. If necessary, start Word, make sure your Data Disk is in the appropriate disk drive, and check your screen to make sure your settings match those in the tutorials.
2. Open the file **Store** from the Tutorial 2 Cases folder on your Data Disk, and save it as **Store-It-All Policies**.
3. Use the Spelling and Grammar checker to correct any errors in the document. Then proofread the document to check for errors the Spelling and Grammar checker missed. Pay particular attention to the paragraph under "Rental Payments" and the company name throughout the document.
4. Delete the word "basic" from the first sentence of the first full paragraph. (Remember to use the Undo and Redo buttons as you work to correct any editing mistakes.)
5. Delete the second sentence in the second paragraph, which begins "You renew your contract… ."
6. Insert the bolded sentence "A bill will not be sent to you." before the first sentence under the heading "Rental Payments."
7. Under the heading "Insurance," delete the sentence in parentheses and the extra paragraph mark.
8. Change all of the margins (top, bottom, left, and right) to 1.75 inches.
9. For each paragraph following a heading, set the alignment to justify. (*Hint:* Format the first paragraph and then use the Format Painter to format each successive paragraph.)
10. Find the phrase "not negotiable" using the Find command and italicize it.
11. Indent the four-item list under the heading "Delinquent Accounts" 0.5-inch and add bullets.
12. Change both lines of the title to 14-point Arial (or another sans serif font of your choice).
13. Center and bold both lines of the title.
14. Underline all of the headings.

15. Insert two blank lines at the end of the document, and then type the following, making sure to replace "*your name*" with your first and last name: Direct all questions to *your name* in the main office.

16. Save, preview, and print the rental information sheet, and close the document.

Case 2. UpTime Matt Patterson is UpTime's marketing director for the Northeast region. The company provides productivity training for large companies across the country. Matt wants to provide interested clients with a one-page summary of UpTime's productivity training.

1. If necessary, start Word, make sure your Data Disk is in the appropriate disk drive, and check your screen to make sure your settings match those in the tutorials.

2. Open the file **UpTime** from the Tutorial 2 Cases folder on your Data Disk, and save it as **UpTime Training Summary**.

3. Change the title at the beginning of the document to a 16-point serif font other than Times New Roman. Be sure to pick a font that looks professional and is easy to read. (Remember to use the Undo and Redo buttons as you work to correct any editing mistakes.)

4. Center and bold the title.

5. Delete the word "general" from the second sentence of the first paragraph after the document title.

6. Convert the list of training components following the first paragraph to an indented, numbered list.

7. Under the heading "Personal Productivity Training Seminar," delete the third sentence from the first paragraph.

8. Under the heading "Personal Productivity Training Seminar," delete the phrase "at the seminar" from the first sentence in the second paragraph.

9. In the first paragraph under the heading "Management Productivity Training," move the first sentence (beginning with "UpTime provides management training…") to the end of the paragraph.

10. Switch the order of the first and second paragraphs under the "Field Services Technology and Training" heading.

11. Search for the text "your name," and replace it with your first and last name.

12. Change the top margin to 1.5 inches.

13. Change the left margin to 1.75 inches.

14. Bold each of the headings.

15. Italicize both occurrences of the word "free" in the second paragraph under the "Field Services Technology and Training" heading.

16. Save and preview the document.

17. Print the document, and then close the file.

Case 3. Ridge Top Thomas McGee is vice president of sales and marketing at Ridge Top, an outdoor and sporting-gear store in Conshohocken, Pennsylvania. Each year, Thomas and his staff mail a description of new products to Ridge Top's regular customers. Ralph has asked you to edit and format the first few pages of this year's new products' description.

1. If necessary, start Word, make sure your Data Disk is in the appropriate disk drive, and check your screen to make sure your settings match those in the tutorials.

2. Open the file **Ridge** from the Tutorial 2 Cases folder on your Data Disk, and save it as **Ridge Top Guide**.

3. Use the Spelling and Grammar checker to correct any errors in the document. Because of the nature of this document, it contains some words that the Word dictionary on your computer may not recognize. It also contains headings that the Spelling and Grammar checker may consider sentence fragments. As you use the Spelling and Grammar checker, use the Ignore All button, if necessary, to skip over brand names. Use the Ignore Rule button to skip over sentence fragments.

4. Delete the phrase "a great deal" from the first sentence of the paragraph below the heading "Snuggle Up to These Prices." (Remember to use the Undo and Redo buttons to correct any editing mistakes as you work.)

5. Reverse the order of the first two paragraphs under the heading, "You'll Eat Up the Prices of This Camp Cooking Gear!"

6. Cut the last sentence of the first full paragraph ("Prices are good through...") from the document. Then move the insertion point to the end of the document, press the Enter key twice, and insert the cut sentence as a new paragraph. Format it in 12-point Arial, and italicize it.

7. Format the Ridge Top tip items as a numbered list.

Explore 8. Reorder the items under the "Ridge Top Tips!" heading by moving the fourth product idea and the following paragraph to the top of the list.

9. Search for the text "your name," and replace with your first and last name.

Explore 10. Experiment with two special paragraph alignment options: first line and hanging. First, select everything from the heading "Ridge Top Guarantees Warmth at Cool Prices" through the paragraph just before the heading "Ridge Top Tips." Next, click Format on the menu bar, click Paragraph, click Indents and Spacing tab, click the Help button in the upper-right corner of the dialog box, click the Special list arrow, and review the information on the special alignment options. Experiment with both the First line and the Hanging options. When you are finished, return the document to its original format by choosing the none option.

11. Justify all the paragraphs in the document. (*Hint:* To select all paragraphs in the document at one time, click Edit on the menu bar, and then click Select All.)

12. Replace all occurrences of "RidgeTop" with "Ridge Top."

13. Apply a 12-point, bold, sans serif font to each of the headings. Be sure to pick a font that looks professional and is easy to read. (*Hint:* Use the Format Painter.)

14. Change the title's font to the same font you used for the headings, except set the size to 16 point.

15. Bold both lines of the title.

16. Underline the names and prices for all of the brandname products in the Trekker's Guide. Make sure you don't underline spaces or periods. (*Hint:* Use the Words only underline style option in the Font dialog box.)

17. Save and preview the document. Print the document, and then close the file.

Case 4. Restaurant Review Your student newspaper has asked you to review four restaurants in your area.

1. If necessary, start Word, make sure your Data Disk is in the appropriate disk drive, and check your screen to make sure your settings match those in the tutorials.

2. Write a brief summary (one to two paragraphs) for each restaurant and provide a rating for each one. Correct any spelling or grammatical errors.

3. Add a title and subtitle to your review. The subtitle should include your name.

4. Save the document as **Restaurant Review** in the Tutorial 2 Cases folder on your Data Disk, and print it.

5. Rearrange the order in which you discuss the restaurants to alphabetical order. (Remember to use the Undo and Redo buttons as you work to correct any editing mistakes.)

6. Change the top margin to 2 inches.

7. Change the left margin to 1.75 inches.

8. Center and bold the title and subtitle.

9. Change the paragraph alignment to justify.

10. Italicize the title of each restaurant.

11. Save the edited document as **Edited Restaurant Review**.

12. Print the document.

13. Save and close your document.

INTERNET ASSIGNMENTS

The purpose of the Internet Assignments is to challenge you to find information on the Internet that you can use to create effective documents. The actual assignments are updated and maintained on the Course Technology Web site. Log on to the Internet and use your Web browser to go to the Student Online Companion to accompany this text at **www.course.com/NewPerspectives/office2000**. Click the Word link, and then click the link for Tutorial 2.

QUICK CHECK ANSWERS

Session 2.1

1. Click the Open button on the Standard toolbar, or click File, click Open, and double-click the file. Click File, click Save As, select the location, type the new filename, and then click OK.
2. (a) $\downarrow$; (b) Ctrl+End; (c) Page Down
3. The process of first selecting the text to be modified, and then performing the operations such as moving, formatting, or deleting.
4. (a) The blank space in the left margin area of the document window, which allows you to easily select entire lines or large blocks of text. (b) The button on the Standard toolbar that redoes an action you previously reversed using the Undo button. (c) The process of moving text by first selecting the text, then pressing and holding the mouse button while moving the text to its new location in the document, and finally releasing the mouse button.
5. To select a single word, double-click the word, or click at the beginning of the word, and drag the pointer to the end of the word. To select a complete paragraph, triple-click in the selection bar next to the paragraph, or click at the beginning of the paragraph and drag the pointer to the end of the paragraph.
6. You might use the Undo button to remove the bold formatting you had just applied to a word. You could then use the Redo button to restore the bold formatting to the word.
7. False
8. Cut and paste removes the selected material from its original location and inserts it in a new location. Copy and paste makes a copy of the selected material and inserts the copy in a new location; the original material remains in its original location.
9. Click the Select Browse Object button, click the Find button, click the Replace tab, type the search text in the Find what text box, type the replacement text in the Replace with text box, click Find Next or click Replace all.

Session 2.2

1. The default top and bottom margins are 1 inch. The default left and right margins are 1.25 inches.
2. Align-left: each line flush left, ragged right.
   Align-right: each line flush right, ragged left.
   Center: each line centered, ragged right and left.
   Justify: each line flush left and flush right.
3. Click in the paragraph you want to indent, and then click the Increase Indent button on the Formatting toolbar once for each half-inch you want to indent.
4. You might use the Format Painter to copy the formatting of a heading with bold italic to the other headings in the document.
5. Click the Underline button on the Formatting toolbar, type the word, and then click the Underline button again to turn off underlining.
6. Select the paragraphs, and then click the Numbering button on the Formatting toolbar.
7. Select the title, click the Font list arrow, and click Arial in the list of fonts. Then click the Font Size list arrow, and click 14.
8. Select the text you want to change, click Format on the menu bar, click Paragraph, click the Line Spacing list arrow, and then click Single, 1.5, or Double. Or, select the text, and then press Ctrl+1 for single spacing, Ctrl+5 for 1.5 line spacing, or Ctrl+2 for double spacing.

OBJECTIVES

In this tutorial you will:

- Set tab stops

- Divide a document into sections

- Change the vertical alignment of a section

- Center a page between the top and bottom margins

- Create a header with page numbers

- Create a table

- Sort the rows in a table

- Modify a table's structure

- Total a column of numbers with AutoSum

- Format a table

CREATING A MULTIPLE-PAGE REPORT

Writing a Recommendation Report for AgriTechnology

CASE

AgriTechnology

Brittany Jones works for AgriTechnology, a biotechnology company that develops genetically engineered food products. Recently, AgriTechnology began shipping the EverRipe tomato to supermarkets. The EverRipe tomato is genetically engineered to stay ripe and fresh nearly twice as long as other varieties. Because of its longer shelf life and vine-ripened taste, the new tomato is popular with supermarkets, and demand for it has been high. Unfortunately, the EverRipe tomato also is more susceptible to bruising than standard varieties. Nearly 20 percent of the first year's crop was unmarketable because of damage sustained during shipping and handling. AgriTechnology's vice president, Ramon Espinoza, appointed Brittany to head a task force to determine how to increase the profitability of the EverRipe. The task force is ready to present the results of their study in the form of a report with an accompanying table. Brittany asks you to help prepare the report.

In this tutorial, you will format the report's title page so that it has a different layout from the rest of the report. The title page will contain only the title and subtitle and will not have page numbers like the rest of the report. You also will add a table to the AgriTechnology report that summarizes the task force's recommendations.

SESSION 3.1

In this session you will review the task force's recommendation report. Then you will learn how to set tab stops, divide a document into sections, center a page between the top and bottom margins, create a header, and create a table.

Planning the Document

As head of the task force, Brittany divided the responsibility for the report among the members of the group. Each person gathered information about one aspect of the problem and wrote the appropriate section of the report. Now, Brittany must compile all the findings into a coherent and unified report. In addition, she also must follow the company's style guidelines for the content, organization, style, and format.

The report content includes the results of the study—obtained from interviews with other employees and visits to the packaging and distribution plant, trucking company, and so forth—and recommendations for action.

Because Brittany knows some executives will not have time to read the entire report, she organized the report so it begins with an executive summary. The body of the report provides an in-depth statement of the problem and recommendations for solving that problem. At the end of the report, she summarizes the cost of the improvements.

The report's style follows established standards of business writing, and emphasizes clarity, simplicity, and directness.

In accordance with AgriTechnology's style guide, Brittany's report will begin with a title page, with the text centered between the top and bottom margins. Every page except the title page will include a line of text at the top, giving a descriptive name for the report, as well as the page number. The text and headings will be formatted to match all AgriTechnology's reports, and will follow company guidelines for layout and text style.

At the end of the report, there will be a table that summarizes the costs of the proposed changes.

Opening the Report

Brittany already has combined the individual sections into one document. She also has begun formatting the report by changing the font size of headings, adding elements such as bold and italics, and by indenting paragraphs. You'll open the document and perform the remaining formatting tasks on page 1, as indicated in Figure 3-1.

| Figure 3-1 | **INITIAL DRAFT OF TASK FORCE'S REPORT WITH EDITS (PAGE 1)** |

Increasing the Profitability of AgriTechnology's EverRipe Tomatoes

Make this a vertically centered title page

Prepared for
Ramon Espinoza, Vice President
AgriTechnology

Set tab stop

Prepared by Task Force Members
Brittany Jones   Marketing Manager
Anthony Ciaccio   Research Associate
Dominic Carmon-Estevon Research Associate
Russell Edgington   Distribution Specialist

Replace with your name

Start new page

Executive Summary

Insert header in this section

Almost 20 percent of the EverRipe tomato crop was unmarketable due to damage sustained during packaging and distribution. This resulted in an estimated loss in profits of $1.2 million. AgriTechnology could increase the percentage of marketable crop and increase profits by upgrading its packaging plants, constructing distribution centers, purchasing trucking facilities, and automating delivery services. Costs for implementing these improvements would be approximately $7.2 million. The company should be able to recoup that investment within four years.

Introduction

This report presents our findings on how to improve the profitability of the EverRipe tomato crop. First, we describe how part of the crop was unmarketable due to loss during packaging and distribution. Then, we recommend improvements to the current packaging and distribution process that will reduce damage to future crops. Finally, we project costs for implementing these changes.

Loss of Profits for 2001

Although these tomatoes are genetically engineered to remain ripe for longer periods of time, they're more easily bruised than conventional tomatoes. AgriTechnology reports indicate that 18.7 percent of this year's crop was unmarketable due to damage sustained during packaging and

To open the document:

1. Start Word, and place your Data Disk in the appropriate drive. Make sure your screen matches the figures in this tutorial. In particular, be sure to display the nonprinting characters.

2. Open the file **EverRipe** from the **Tutorial** folder in the **Tutorial.03** folder on your Data Disk.

3. To avoid altering the original file, save the document as **EverRipe Report** in the same folder.

4. In the first page, replace the name "Russell Edgington" with your name.

Setting Tab Stops

Tabs are useful for indenting paragraphs and for vertically aligning text or numerical data in columns. A **tab** adds space between the margin and text in a column or between text in one column and text in another column. A **tab stop** is the location where text moves when you press the Tab key. When the Show/Hide ¶ button is pressed, the nonprinting tab character → appears wherever you press the Tab key. A tab character is just like any other character you type; you can delete it by pressing the Backspace key or the Delete key.

Word provides several **tab-stop alignment styles**. The five major styles are left, center, right, decimal, and bar, as shown in Figure 3-2. The first three tab-stop styles position text in a similar way to the Align Left, Center, and Align Right buttons on the Formatting tool-bar. The difference is that with a tab, you determine line by line precisely where the left, center, or right alignment should occur.

Figure 3-2	TAB STOP ALIGNMENT STYLES

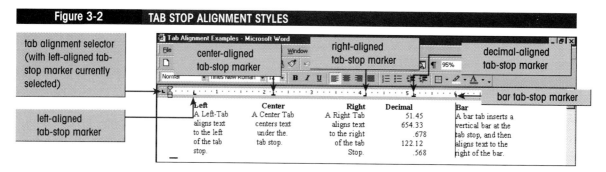

The default tab stops on the ruler are **Left tabs**, which position the left edge of text at the tab stop and extend the text to the right. **Center tabs** position text so that it's centered evenly on both sides of the tab stop. **Right tabs** position the right edge of text at the tab stop and extend the text to the left. **Decimal tabs** position numbers so that their decimal points are aligned at the tab stop. **Bar tabs** insert a vertical bar at the tab stop and then align text to the right of the bar. In addition, you also can use a **First Line Indent tab**, which indents the first line of a paragraph, and the **Hanging Indent tab**, which indents every line of a paragraph *except* the first line.

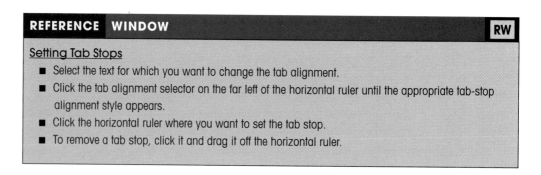

REFERENCE WINDOW   **RW**

Setting Tab Stops

- Select the text for which you want to change the tab alignment.
- Click the tab alignment selector on the far left of the horizontal ruler until the appropriate tab-stop alignment style appears.
- Click the horizontal ruler where you want to set the tab stop.
- To remove a tab stop, click it and drag it off the horizontal ruler.

The Word default tab-stop settings are every one-half inch, as indicated by the small gray ticks at the bottom of the ruler shown in Figure 3-3. You set a new tab stop by selecting a tab-stop alignment style (from the tab alignment selector at the left end of the horizontal ruler) and then clicking on the horizontal ruler to insert the tab stop. You can remove a tab stop from the ruler by clicking it and dragging the tab stop off the ruler.

Figure 3-3	RULER WITH TAB STOPS

ruler

You should never try to align columns of text by adding extra spaces with the spacebar. Although the text might seem precisely aligned in the document window, it might not be aligned when you print the document. Furthermore, if you edit the text, the extra spaces might disturb the alignment. However, if you edit text aligned with tabs, the alignment remains intact. If you want to align a lot of text in many columns, it is better to use a table, as described later in this tutorial.

To align columns using tabs, you can type some text, and press the Tab key. The insertion point will then move to the next tab stop to the right, where you can type more text. You can continue in this way until you have typed the first row of each column. Then you can press the Enter key, and begin typing the next row of each column.

However, sometimes you'll find that text in a column stretches beyond the next default tab stop, and as a result the columns will fail to line up evenly. In this situation, you need to set new tab stops on the horizontal ruler. For example, even though the list of task force members in the EverRipe report contains tab stops, the columns do not line up evenly. To fix this formatting problem, you need to move the tab stop farther to the right.

To add a new tab stop on the ruler:

1. Make sure the current tab-stop alignment style is left tab **L**, as shown in Figure 3-3. If **L** doesn't appear at that location, click the tab alignment selector one or more times until **L** appears.

2. Select the list of task force members and their titles on page 1. (Do not select the heading "Prepared by Task Force Members.")

3. Click the tick mark on the ruler that occurs at 3.0 inches. Word automatically inserts a left tab stop at that location and removes the tick marks to its left. The second column of text shifts to the new tab stop.

4. Deselect the highlighted text and then move the insertion point anywhere in the list of names and titles. See Figure 3-4.

| Figure 3-4 | LEFT TAB STOP ON RULER |

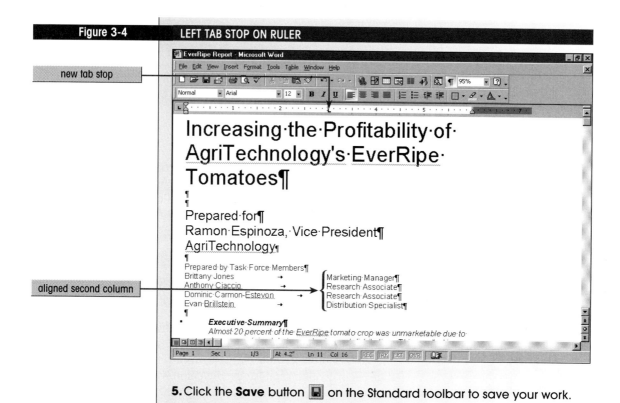

new tab stop

aligned second column

5. Click the **Save** button 🔲 on the Standard toolbar to save your work.

The two columns of information are now aligned, as Brittany requested. Notice that Word changed the tab stops only for the selected paragraphs, not for all the paragraphs in the document. You set the other tabs the same way. Next, you need to change the layout of the title page.

Formatting the Document in Sections

According to the company guidelines, the title page of the report should be centered between the top and bottom margins of the page. In order to format the title page differently from the rest of the report, you need to divide the document into sections. A **section** is a unit or part of a document that can have its own page orientation, margins, headers, footers, and vertical alignment. Each section, in other words, is like a mini-document within a document.

To divide a document into sections, you insert a **section break** (a dotted line with the words "End of Section") that marks the point at which one section ends and another begins. Sections can start on a new page or continue on the same page. You can insert a section break with the Break command on the Insert menu.

To insert a section break after the title:

1. Position the insertion point immediately to the left of the "E" in the heading "Executive Summary." You want the text above this heading to be on a separate title page and the executive summary to begin the second page of the report.

2. Click **Insert** on the menu bar, and then click **Break** to open the Break dialog box. See Figure 3-5.

Figure 3-5	BREAK DIALOG BOX

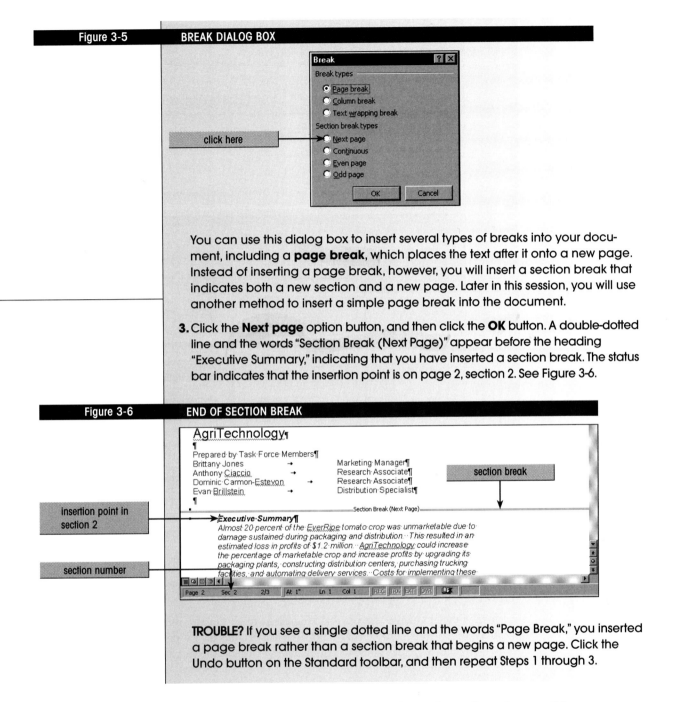

You can use this dialog box to insert several types of breaks into your document, including a **page break**, which places the text after it onto a new page. Instead of inserting a page break, however, you will insert a section break that indicates both a new section and a new page. Later in this session, you will use another method to insert a simple page break into the document.

3. Click the **Next page** option button, and then click the **OK** button. A double-dotted line and the words "Section Break (Next Page)" appear before the heading "Executive Summary," indicating that you have inserted a section break. The status bar indicates that the insertion point is on page 2, section 2. See Figure 3-6.

Figure 3-6	END OF SECTION BREAK

TROUBLE? If you see a single dotted line and the words "Page Break," you inserted a page break rather than a section break that begins a new page. Click the Undo button on the Standard toolbar, and then repeat Steps 1 through 3.

Now that the title page is a separate section and page from the rest of the report, you can make changes affecting only that section, leaving the rest of the document unchanged.

Changing the Vertical Alignment of a Section

You're ready to center the text of page one vertically on the page. But first, you will switch to the Print Preview window, so you can more easily observe your changes to page one.

To see the document in Print Preview:

1. Click the **Print Preview** button 🔍 on the Standard toolbar to open the Print Preview window.

2. Click the **Multiple Pages** button 🔡 on the Print Preview toolbar, and then click and drag across the top three pages in the list box to select "1 x 3 Pages." The three pages of the report are reduced in size and appear side-by-side. See Figure 3-7. Although you cannot read the text on the pages, you can see the general layout.

Figure 3-7   **PRINT PREVIEW OF REPORT**

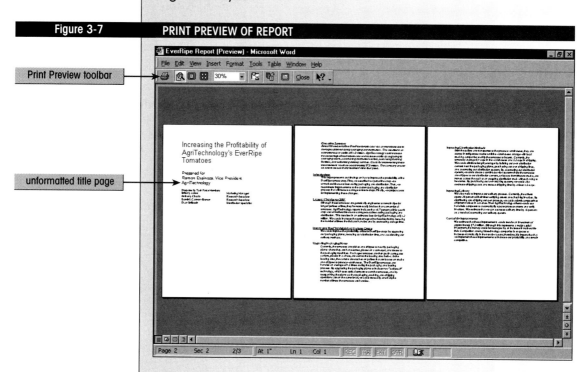

Print Preview toolbar

unformatted title page

TROUBLE? If you see the vertical and horizontal rulers, you can click the View Ruler button on the Print Preview toolbar to hide the rulers.

Now, you can change the vertical alignment to center the lines of text between the top and bottom margins. The **vertical alignment** specifies how a page of text is positioned on the page between the top and bottom margins—flush at the top, flush at the bottom, or centered between the top and bottom margins.

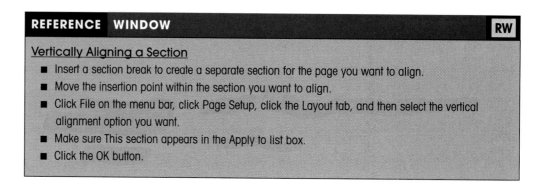

REFERENCE WINDOW   **RW**

Vertically Aligning a Section
- Insert a section break to create a separate section for the page you want to align.
- Move the insertion point within the section you want to align.
- Click File on the menu bar, click Page Setup, click the Layout tab, and then select the vertical alignment option you want.
- Make sure This section appears in the Apply to list box.
- Click the OK button.

You'll center the title page text from within the Print Preview window.

To change the vertical alignment of the title page:

1. If the **Magnifier** button is selected, click it once to deselect it.

2. Click the leftmost page in the Print Preview window to make sure the current page is page 1 (the title page). The status bar in the Print Preview window indicates the current page.

3. Click **File** on the menu bar, and then click **Page Setup**. The Page Setup dialog box opens.

4. Click the **Layout** tab. In the Apply to list box, click **This section** (if it is not already selected) so that the layout change affects only the first section, not both sections, of your document.

5. Click the **Vertical alignment** list arrow, and then click **Center** to center the pages of the current section—in this case, just page 1—vertically between the top and bottom margins.

6. Click the **OK** button to return to the Print Preview window. The text of the title page is centered vertically, as shown in Figure 3-8.

| Figure 3-8 | TITLE PAGE VERTICALLY CENTERED |

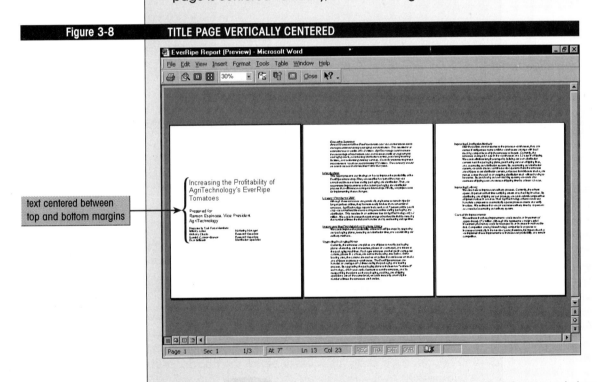

text centered between top and bottom margins

7. Click the **Close** button on the Print Preview toolbar to return to normal view.

You have successfully centered the title page text. Next you turn your attention to placing a descriptive name for the report and the page number at the top of every page.

Adding **Headers**

The AgriTechnology report guidelines require a short report title and the page number to be printed at the top of every page except the title page. Text that is printed at the top of every page is called a **header**. For example, the page number, tutorial number, and tutorial name printed at the top of the page you are reading is a header. Similarly, a **footer** is text that is printed at the bottom of every page. (You'll have a chance to work with footers in the Review Assignments at the end of this tutorial.)

When you insert a header or footer into a document, you switch to Header and Footer view. The Header and Footer toolbar is displayed, and the insertion point moves to the top of the document, where the header will appear. The main text is dimmed, indicating that it cannot be edited until you return to normal or print layout view.

REFERENCE WINDOW   **RW**

<u>Inserting a Header or Footer</u>
- Click View on the menu bar, and then click Header and Footer.
- Type the text for the header. The header will appear in all subsequent pages.
- To insert a footer, click the Switch Between Header and Footer button on the Header and Footer toolbar.
- To create different headers for odd and even pages, click the Page Setup button on the Header and Footer toolbar, click the Layout tab, and then select the Different odd and even check box. To create a different header or footer for the first page of the document or section, select the Different first page check box. Click OK.
- Click the Close button on the Header and Footer toolbar.

You'll create a header for the main body of the report (section 2) that prints "EverRipe Recommendation Report" at the left margin and the page number at the right margin.

To insert a header for section 2:

1. Make sure the insertion point is positioned after the heading "Executive Summary" on page 2 so that the insertion point is in section 2 and not in section 1.

2. Click **View** on the menu bar, and then click **Header and Footer**. The screen changes to Header and Footer view, and the Header and Footer toolbar appears in the document window. The header area appears in the top margin of your document surrounded by a dashed line and displays the words "Header -Section 2-." See Figure 3-9. (If the Header and Footer toolbar covers the header area, drag the toolbar below the header area, similar to its position in Figure 3-9.)

Figure 3-9	CREATING A HEADER

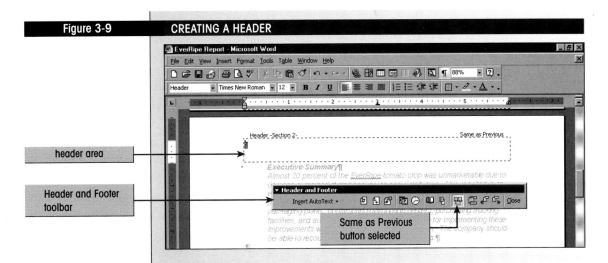

header area

Header and Footer toolbar

Same as Previous button selected

TROUBLE? If the header area displays "Header -Section 1-," click the Show Next button on the Header and Footer toolbar until the header area displays "Header -Section 2-."

TROUBLE? If the main text of the document doesn't appear on the screen, click the Show/Hide Document Text button on the Header and Footer toolbar, and continue with Step 3.

3. Click the **Same as Previous** button on the Header and Footer toolbar so that the button is *not* selected. When Same as Previous is selected, Word automatically inserts the same header text as the previous section. You deselected it to ensure that the text of the current header will apply only to the current section (section 2), not to the previous section (section 1) also.

4. Type **EverRipe Recommendation Report**. The title is automatically aligned on the left. See Figure 3-10.

Figure 3-10	TEXT OF HEADER

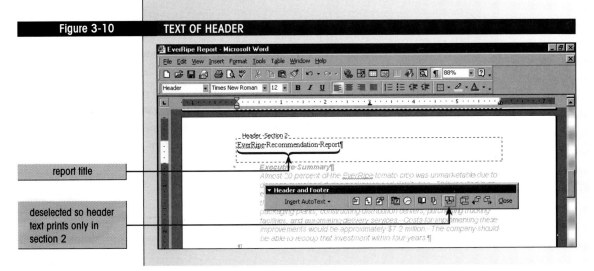

report title

deselected so header text prints only in section 2

5. Press the **Tab** key twice to move the insertion point to the right margin of the header area. (Notice that by default the header contains a center and right-align tab stop.)

6. Type the word **Page** and press the **spacebar** once.

7. Click the **Insert Page Number** button on the Header and Footer toolbar. The page number "2" appears at the right-aligned tab.

The page number in the header looks like you simply typed the number 2, but you actually inserted a special instruction telling Word to insert the correct page number on each page. Now consecutive page numbers will print on each page of the header within this section.

8. Click the **Close** button on the Header and Footer toolbar to return to normal view, and then save your changes.

Notice that you can't see the header in normal view. To see exactly how the header will appear on the printed page, you will switch to print layout view, which lets you read the headers and footers as well as see the margins.

To view the header and margins in print layout view:

1. Click the **Print Layout View** button . You can now see the header and the page margins. Next, you'll use the browse buttons to examine each page. Begin by using the Select Browse Object button to select the feature, or object, you want to browse for. In this case, you will browse by page.

2. Click the **Select Browse Object** button below the vertical scroll bar and click the **Browse by Page** button . The insertion point moves to the top of the third page. Now that you've selected the browse object (page), you can use the Next and Previous buttons to move quickly from one page to the next.

3. Click the **Previous Page** button (just above the Select Browse Object button) twice to move to page 1.

4. Click the **Next Page** button (just below the Select Browse Object button) to move to the top of page 2.

5. Click again to move to the top of page 3. Notice that the header appears only on pages 2 and 3. The header does not appear on the title page because the title page is in a different section of the document. Also notice that the correct page numbers appear on pages 2 and 3. See Figure 3-11.

| Figure 3-11 | HEADER IN PRINT LAYOUT VIEW |

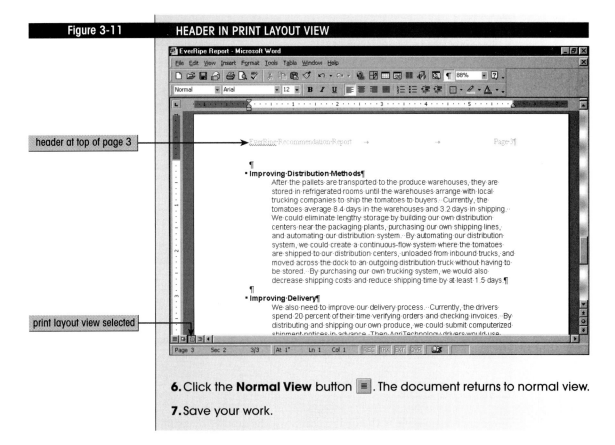

header at top of page 3

print layout view selected

6. Click the **Normal View** button ▤. The document returns to normal view.

7. Save your work.

The recommendation report now has the required header. You have formatted Brittany's recommendation report so that the results are professional-looking, clearly presented, and easy to read. Next you will add a table that summarizes the costs and benefits of the task force's recommendations.

Inserting Tables

You can quickly organize data and arrange text in an easy-to-read table format. A **table** is information arranged in horizontal rows and vertical columns. As shown in Figure 3-12, table rows are commonly referred to by number (row 1 at the top, row 2 below row 1, and so forth), while columns are commonly referred to by letter (column A on the far left, column B to the right of column A, and so forth). However, you do not see row and column numbers on the screen. The area where a row and column intersect is called a **cell**. Each cell is identified by a column and row label. For example, the cell in the upper-left corner of a table is cell A1 (column A, row 1), the cell to the right of that is cell B1, the cell below cell A1 is A2, and so forth. The table's structure is shown by **gridlines**, which are light gray lines that define the rows and columns. By default, gridlines do not appear on the printed page. You can emphasize specific parts of a table on the printed page by adding a **border** (a line the prints along the side of a table cell). When you move the pointer over a table that is displayed in print layout view, the Table move handle and the Table resize handle appear. To quickly select the entire table, click the **Table move handle**. Then you can drag the Table move handle to move the table to a new location. To change the size of the entire table, drag the **Table resize handle**.

Figure 3-12 **ELEMENTS OF A WORD TABLE**

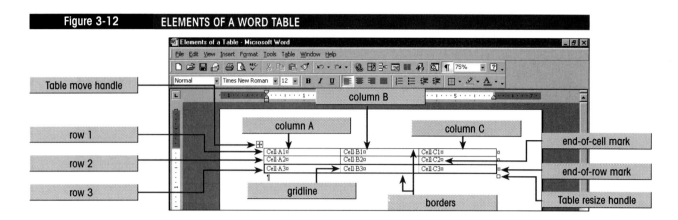

With the Word Table feature you can create a blank table and then insert information into it (as you'll do next), or you can convert existing text into a table (as you'll do in the Review Assignments).

You may be wondering why you can't use tabs to align text in columns. Tabs work well for smaller amounts of information, such as two or three columns with three or four rows, but tabs and columns become tedious and difficult to work with when you need to organize a larger amount of more complex information. The Word Table feature allows you to quickly organize data and to place text and graphics in a more readable format.

Creating a Table

You can create a table with equal column widths quickly by using the Insert Table button on the Standard toolbar. (You will use this technique to create the table Brittany requested.) You also can create a table by dragging the Draw Table pointer to draw the table structure you want. (You'll practice this method in the Case Problems.) However you create a table, you can modify it by using commands on the Table menu or the buttons on the Tables and Borders toolbar.

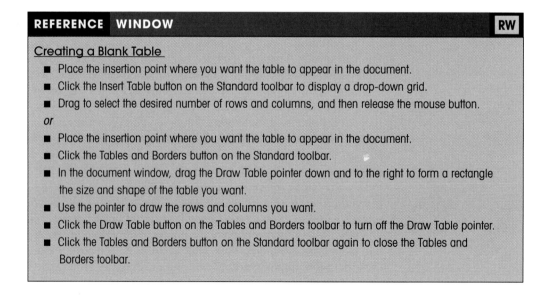

REFERENCE WINDOW   **RW**

__Creating a Blank Table__
- Place the insertion point where you want the table to appear in the document.
- Click the Insert Table button on the Standard toolbar to display a drop-down grid.
- Drag to select the desired number of rows and columns, and then release the mouse button.

or

- Place the insertion point where you want the table to appear in the document.
- Click the Tables and Borders button on the Standard toolbar.
- In the document window, drag the Draw Table pointer down and to the right to form a rectangle the size and shape of the table you want.
- Use the pointer to draw the rows and columns you want.
- Click the Draw Table button on the Tables and Borders toolbar to turn off the Draw Table pointer.
- Click the Tables and Borders button on the Standard toolbar again to close the Tables and Borders toolbar.

Brittany wants you to create a table that summarizes information in the EverRipe report. Figure 3-13 shows a sketch of what Brittany wants the table to look like. The table will allow AgriTechnology's executives to see at a glance the cost and benefit of each improvement.

Figure 3-13	SKETCH OF EVERRIPE TABLE

Projected Improvement	Benefit	Percent of Total Cost	Initial Cost
Upgrade packaging plants	Reduce by one-half the number of times tomatoes are handled	21%	$1,000,000
Administrative improvements	Facilitate transition to new system	.2%	$200,000
Improve distribution methods	Decrease shipping costs and reduce shipping time by 1.5 days	51%	$3,700,000
Automate delivery paperwork	Decrease delivery time by 15%	35%	$2,500,000

Before you begin creating the table, you insert a page break so that the table will appear on a separate page.

To insert a page break:

1. Press **Ctrl+End** to position the insertion point at the end of the last paragraph in the report.

2. Press **Ctrl+Enter**. A dotted line with the words "Page Break" appears in the document window. (Note that you also could add a page break using the Break dialog box you used earlier to insert a section break.)

   TROUBLE? If you do not see the words "Page Break," check to make sure the document is displayed in normal view.

The insertion point is now at the beginning of a new page, where you want to insert the table. You'll use the Insert Table button to create the table.

To create a blank table using the Insert Table button:

1. Click the **Insert Table** button 🔲 on the Standard toolbar. A drop-down grid resembling a miniature table appears below the Insert Table button. The grid initially has four rows and five columns. You can drag the pointer to extend the grid to as many rows and columns as you need. In this case, you need five rows and four columns.

2. Position the pointer in the upper-left cell of the grid, and then click and drag the pointer down and across the grid until you highlight five rows and four columns. As you drag the pointer across the grid, Word indicates the size of the table (rows by columns) at the bottom of the grid. See Figure 3-14.

| Figure 3-14 | SELECTING ROWS AND COLUMNS |

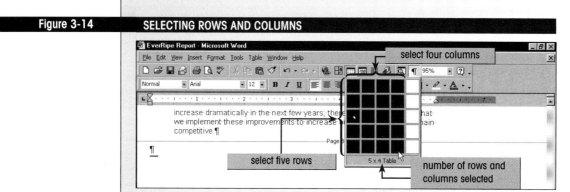

3. Release the mouse button. An empty table, five rows by four columns, appears in your document with the insertion point blinking in the upper-left corner (cell A1). See Figure 3-15.

| Figure 3-15 | EMPTY TABLE INSERTED INTO DOCUMENT |

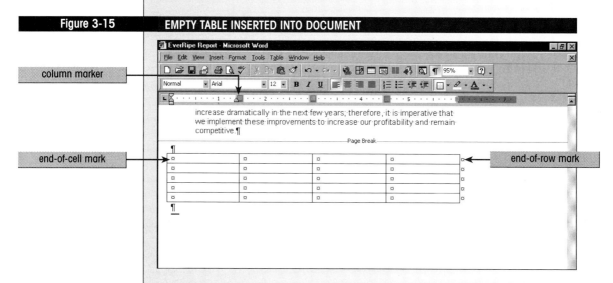

The table is outlined with borders, and the four columns are of equal width. The column widths are indicated by column markers on the ruler. Each cell contains an end-of-cell mark, and each row contains an end-of-row mark.

TROUBLE? If you don't see the end-of-cell and end-of-row marks, you need to show nonprinting characters. Click the Show/Hide ¶ button on the Standard toolbar to show nonprinting characters.

TROUBLE? If you see the Tables and Borders toolbar displayed along with the new blank table, simply continue with this tutorial. You will learn how to use the Tables and Borders toolbar in the next session.

Entering Text in a Table

You can enter text in a table by moving the insertion point to a cell and typing. If the text takes up more than one line in the cell, Word automatically wraps the text to the next line and increases the height of that cell and all the cells in that row. To move the insertion point to another cell in the table, you can either click in that cell or use the Tab key. Figure 3-16 summarizes the keystrokes for moving within a table.

Figure 3-16	KEYSTROKES FOR MOVING AROUND A TABLE

PRESS	TO MOVE THE INSERTION POINT
Tab or →	One cell to the right, or to the first cell in the next row.
Shift+Tab or ←	One cell to the left, or to the last cell in the previous row.
Alt+Home	To first cell of current row.
Alt+End	To last cell of current row.
Alt+PageUp	To top cell of current column.
Alt+PageDown	To bottom cell of current column.
↑	One cell up in current column.
↓	One cell down in current column.

Now, you are ready to insert information into the table.

To insert data into the table:

1. Verify that the insertion point is located in cell **A1** (in the upper-left corner).

2. Type **Projected Improvement**.

3. Press the **Tab** key to move to cell B1. See Figure 3-17.

Figure 3-17	ADDING TEXT TO THE TABLE

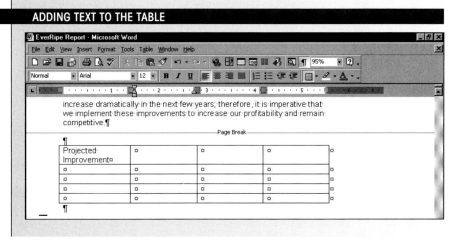

TROUBLE? If Word created a new paragraph in cell A1 rather than moving the insertion point to cell B1, you accidentally pressed the Enter key instead of the Tab key. Press the Backspace key to remove the paragraph mark, and then press the Tab key to move to cell B1.

4. Type **Benefit**, and then press the **Tab** key to move to cell C1.

5. Type **Percent of Total Cost**, and then press the **Tab** key to move to cell D1.

6. Type **Initial Cost**, and then press the **Tab** key to move the insertion point from cell D1 to cell A2. Notice that when you press the Tab key in the last column of the table, the insertion point moves to the first column in the next row.

You have entered the **heading row**, the row that identifies the information in each column.

7. Type the remaining information for the table, as shown in Figure 3-18, pressing the **Tab** key to move from cell to cell. Don't worry if the text in your table doesn't wrap the same way as shown here. You'll change the column widths in the next session.

Figure 3-18	TABLE WITH COMPLETED INFORMATION

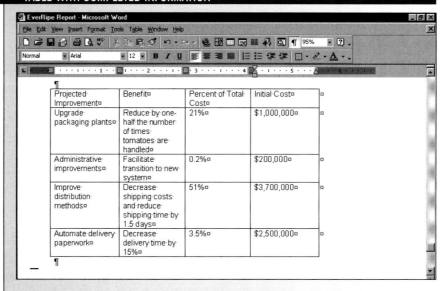

TROUBLE? If a new row (row 6) appeared in your table, you pressed the Tab key when the insertion point was in cell D5, the last cell in the table. Click the Undo button on the Standard toolbar to remove row 6 from the table.

You've now completed a substantial amount of work on the report document, so you decide to save the document with a new name. That way, if for some reason the current document becomes corrupted, you still will have a previous version.

8. Save the document as **EverRipe Report Copy 2** in the **Tutorial** folder of the **Tutorial.03** folder.

Keep in mind that many document-editing features, such as the Backspace key, the copy-and-paste feature, the Undo button, and the AutoCorrect feature, work the same way in a table. Just like in a paragraph, you must select text within a table in order to edit it. You will edit and format this table in the next session.

Session 3.1 QUICK CHECK

1. Define the following in your own words:

   a. tab stop
   b. cell
   c. table
   d. decimal-aligned tab stop
   e. section (of a document)

2. Explain how to center the title page vertically between the top and bottom margins.

3. What is the difference between a header and a footer?

4. Describe how to insert a blank table consisting of four columns and six rows.

5. How do you move the insertion point from one row to the next in a table?

6. How do you insert the page number in a header?

7. Explain how to insert a new tab stop.

8. Describe a situation in which you would want to divide a document into sections.

9. Describe a situation in which it would be better to use a table rather than tab stops.

10. Explain how to select an entire table.

SESSION 3.2

In this session you will learn how to make changes to the table you just created. First you will rearrange the existing rows, and then you will learn how to add and delete rows. Next you will use the AutoSum feature to total a column of numbers, and then format the table to improve its appearance. You also will learn how to merge and split cells as well as how to rotate text within a cell.

Sorting Rows in a Table

The term **sort** refers to the process of rearranging information in alphabetical, numerical, or chronological order. When you sort a table, you arrange the rows based on the contents of one of the columns. For example, you could sort the table you just created based on the contents of the Projected Improvement column—either in ascending alphabetical order (from A to Z) or in descending alphabetical order (from Z to A). Alternatively, you could sort the table based on the contents of the Initial Cost column—either in descending numerical order (highest to lowest) or in ascending numerical order (lowest to highest). When you sort table data, Word usually does not sort the heading row along with the other information, but instead leaves the heading row at the top of the table.

The easiest way to sort a table is to use the Sort buttons on the **Tables and Borders toolbar**. You'll display the Tables and Borders toolbar in the following steps. As you will see, it contains a number of useful buttons that simplify the process of working with tables.

1. If you took a break after the last session, make sure Word is running and that the EverRipe Report Copy 2 document is open. Check that the nonprinting characters are displayed and that the document is displayed in normal view.

2. Right-click the **Standard toolbar**, and then click **Tables and Borders** in the shortcut menu. The Tables and Borders toolbar appears.

3. If necessary, drag the Tables and Borders toolbar down and to the right, so that it doesn't block your view of the EverRipe table. See Figure 3-19.

Figure 3-19	TABLE AND BORDERS TOOLBAR

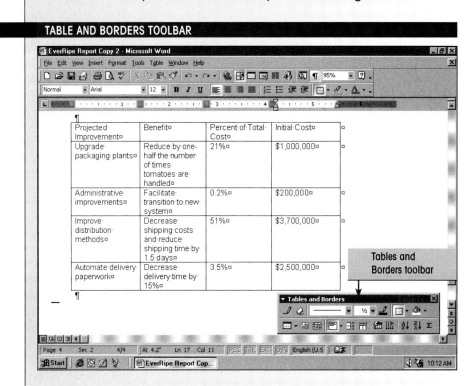

Brittany would like you to sort the table in ascending numerical order, based on the contents of the Initial Cost column. You start by positioning the insertion point in that column.

To sort the information in the table:

1. Click cell **D2** (which contains the value $1,000,000). The insertion point is now located in the Initial Cost column.

2. Click the **Sort Ascending** button on the Tables and Borders toolbar. Rows 2 through 5 now are arranged numerically from the lowest to the highest according to the numbers in the Initial Cost column. See Figure 3-20.

Figure 3-20 TABLE AFTER BEING SORTED

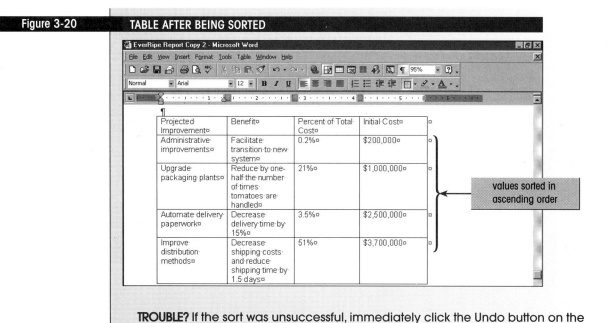

Projected Improvement¤	Benefit¤	Percent of Total Cost¤	Initial Cost¤	¤
Administrative improvements¤	Facilitate transition to new system¤	0.2%¤	$200,000¤	¤
Upgrade packaging plants¤	Reduce by one-half the number of times tomatoes are handled¤	21%¤	$1,000,000¤	¤
Automate delivery paperwork¤	Decrease delivery time by 15%¤	3.5%¤	$2,500,000¤	¤
Improve distribution methods¤	Decrease shipping costs and reduce shipping time by 1.5 days¤	51%¤	$3,700,000¤	¤

values sorted in ascending order

TROUBLE? If the sort was unsuccessful, immediately click the Undo button on the Standard toolbar, and then repeat Steps 1 and 2 to retry the sort.

Brittany stops by and asks you to delete the "Administrative improvements" row because it represents such a small percentage of the total cost. She also would like you to insert a new row to display the total of the Initial Cost column. You'll need to modify the structure of the table in order to complete these tasks.

Modifying an Existing Table Structure

Often, after you create a table, you'll need to delete extra rows and columns or insert additional ones. Figure 3-21 summarizes ways to insert or delete rows and columns in a table.

Figure 3-21 WAYS TO INSERT OR DELETE TABLE ROWS AND COLUMNS

TO	DO THIS
Insert a row within a table	Select the row below where you want the row added, click Table on the menu bar, point to Insert, and then click Rows Above.
	Select the row below where you want the row added, and then click the Insert Rows button on the Standard toolbar.
Insert a row at the end of a table	Position the insertion point in the rightmost cell of the bottom row, and then press the Tab key.
Insert a column within a table	Select the column to the right of where you want the column added, click Table on the menu bar, point to Insert, and then click Columns to the Right.
	Select the column to the right of where you want the column added, and then click the Insert Columns button on the Standard toolbar.
Insert a column at the end of a table	Select the end-of-row markers to the right of the table, click Table on the menu bar, point to Insert, and then click Columns to the Left.
	Select the end-of-row markers to the right of the table, and then click the Insert Columns button on the Standard toolbar.
Delete a row	Select the row or rows to be deleted, click Table on the menu bar, point to Delete, and then click Rows.
Delete a column	Select the column or columns to be deleted, click Table on the menu bar, point to Delete, and then click Columns.

Deleting Rows and Columns in a Table

With Word, you can delete either the contents of the cells or the structure of the cells. To delete the contents of the cells in a selected row, you press the Delete key. However, to delete both the contents and structure of a selected row or column from the table entirely, you must use one of the methods described in Figure 3-21.

To delete a row using the Table menu:

1. Click the selection bar next to row 2 to select the Administrative improvements row.

2. Click **Table** on the menu bar, point to **Delete**, and then click **Rows**. The selected row is deleted from the table structure. See Figure 3-22.

| Figure 3-22 | TABLE AFTER DELETING ROW |

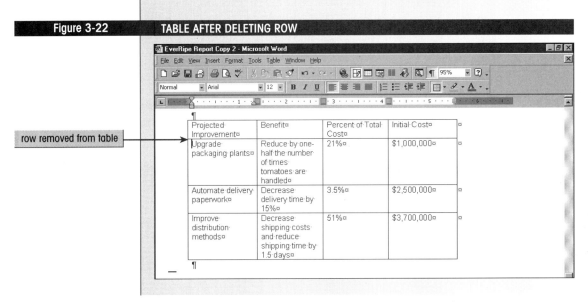

row removed from table

Inserting Additional Rows in a Table

You can insert additional rows within the table or at the end of a table. You now need to insert a row at the bottom of the table, so you can include the total of the Initial Cost column.

To insert a row at the bottom of the table:

1. Click cell **D4**, the last cell of the last row in the table, which contains the number "$3,700,000."

2. Press the **Tab** key. A blank row is added to the bottom of the table.

   TROUBLE? If a blank row is not added to the bottom of the table, click the Undo button on the Standard toolbar. Check to make sure the insertion point is in the last cell of the last row, and then press the Tab key.

3. Type **Total** in cell A5.

You are nearly ready to insert the total of the Initial Cost column in cell D5. First, you need to make it clear that the "Total" heading only applies to the Initial Cost column. You can do that by combining cell A5 with cells at the bottom of the Benefit and Percent of Total Cost columns.

Merging Cells

In addition to adding and deleting rows and columns, you also can change the structure of a table by changing the structure of individual cells. Specifically, you can combine, or **merge**, cells. You also can **split** one cell into multiple rows or columns.

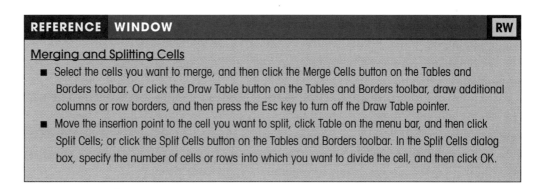

> **REFERENCE WINDOW**   **RW**
>
> **Merging and Splitting Cells**
> - Select the cells you want to merge, and then click the Merge Cells button on the Tables and Borders toolbar. Or click the Draw Table button on the Tables and Borders toolbar, draw additional columns or row borders, and then press the Esc key to turn off the Draw Table pointer.
> - Move the insertion point to the cell you want to split, click Table on the menu bar, and then click Split Cells; or click the Split Cells button on the Tables and Borders toolbar. In the Split Cells dialog box, specify the number of cells or rows into which you want to divide the cell, and then click OK.

You decide to merge cells A5, B5, and C5 to avoid the impression that you intend to insert totals at the bottom of the Benefit column or the Percent of Total Cost column.

To merge cells A5, B5, and C5:

1. Click cell **A5** (containing the word "Total") and drag the pointer to cells **B5** and **C5**. The three cells are now selected.

2. Click the **Merge Cells** button 🔲 on the Tables and Borders toolbar, and then click anywhere within the table to deselect the cells. The borders between the three cells disappear. The three cells are now one, as shown in Figure 3-23.

Figure 3-23   MERGED CELL

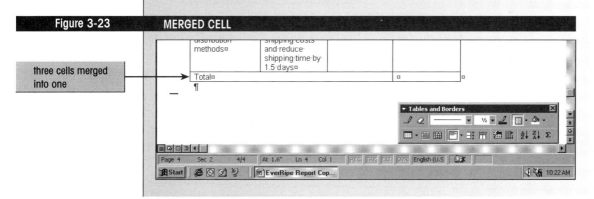

three cells merged into one

Eventually you need to format the text "Total" so that it is aligned next to the Initial Cost column. You will do that later in this tutorial, when you align the percentage values in column C. Now you are ready to calculate the total of the Initial Cost column.

Using AutoSum to Total a Table Column

Rather than calculating column totals by hand and entering them, you can have Word compute the totals of numeric columns in a table. The **AutoSum** feature automatically totals a column of numbers. Note that if you edit any number in the column, you need to click the cell containing the formula, and then press the F9 key to recalculate the total.

To total the values in the Initial Cost column:

1. Click the bottom cell in the Initial Cost column.

2. Click the **AutoSum** button Σ on the Tables and Borders toolbar. The total of the column appears in the cell formatted with a dollar sign and two decimal places. Although you see a number ($7,200,000.00), the cell contains a formula that calculates the total of all the numbers in the column. You can change the way the total looks by formatting the formula. In this case, you want to remove the decimal point and the two zeros.

3. Click the total to select it. The total becomes highlighted in gray.

4. Click **Table** on the menu bar, and then click **Formula**. The Formula dialog box opens.

5. Click the **Number format** list arrow, and select the only format with a dollar sign. You'll remove the part of the formula that specifies how to format negative numbers as well as the decimal codes.

6. In the Number format text box, click to the right of the format and press the **Backspace** key until only $#, ##0 remains, as shown in Figure 3-24.

Figure 3-24 **FORMULA DIALOG BOX AFTER ADJUSTING NUMBER FORMAT**

Formula
Formula:
=SUM(ABOVE)

Number format:
$#,##0

Paste function: Paste bookmark:

Formula
revised number format

7. Click **OK**. The Initial Cost total is now formatted like the numbers above it.

You have finished creating the table, entering data, and modifying the table's structure. Now, you can concentrate on improving the table's appearance.

Formatting Tables

Word provides a variety of ways to enhance the appearance of the tables you create: You can alter the width of the columns and the height of the rows, or change the alignment of text within the cells or the alignment of the table between the left and right margins. You also can change the appearance of the table borders, add a shaded background, and rotate the text within cells.

Changing Column Width and Row Height

Sometimes, you'll want to adjust the column widths in a table to make the text easier to read. If you want to specify an exact width for a column, you should use the Table Properties command on the Table menu. However, it's usually easiest to drag the column's right border to a new position. Note that when adjusting columns and rows, you should switch to print layout view so that the vertical ruler is displayed.

The Percent of Total Cost column (column C) is too wide for the information it contains and should be narrowed. The values in the Initial Cost column look crowded and would be easier to read if the column were wider. You'll change these widths by dragging the column borders, using the ruler as a guide. Keep in mind that to change the width of a column, you need to drag the column's rightmost border.

To change the width of columns by dragging the borders:

1. Switch to print layout view.

2. Position the insertion point anywhere in the EverRipe table (without selecting any text or cells) and then move the pointer over the table without clicking. Notice that in print layout view, the Table move handle and the Table resize handle appear whenever you move the pointer over the table. You will learn more about these two handles in the Review Assignments at the end of this tutorial.

3. Move the pointer over the border between columns C and D (in other words, over the right border of column C, the Percent of Total Cost column). The pointer changes to ↔.

4. Press and hold down the **Alt** key and the mouse button. The column widths are displayed in the ruler, as shown in Figure 3-25.

| Figure 3-25 | COLUMN WIDTHS DISPLAYED IN RULER |

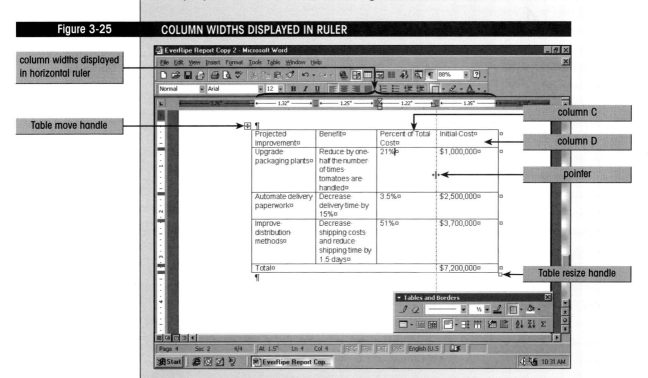

5. While holding down the **Alt** key, drag the pointer to the left until column C (the Percent of Total Cost column) is about **0.75** inches wide, and then release the mouse button. Notice that column C decreases in width and the width of column D (the Initial Cost column) increases. However, the overall width of the table does not change. See Figure 3-26.

Figure 3-26 TABLE AFTER DECREASING THE WIDTH OF COLUMN C

column C reduced to 0.75 inches

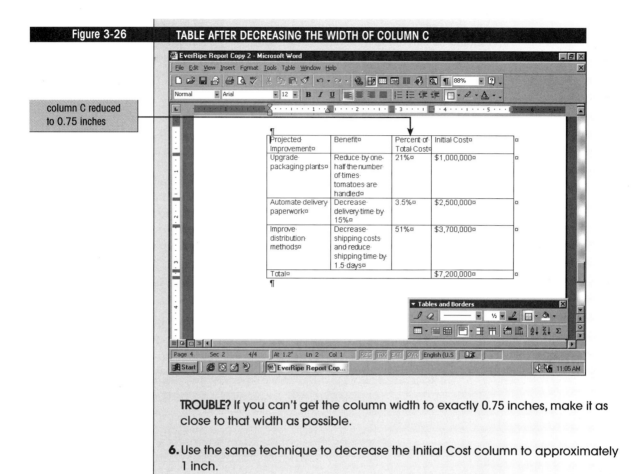

TROUBLE? If you can't get the column width to exactly 0.75 inches, make it as close to that width as possible.

6. Use the same technique to decrease the Initial Cost column to approximately 1 inch.

You also can change the height of rows by dragging a border. You'll make row 1 (the header row) taller so it is more prominent.

To change the height of row 1:

1. Position the pointer over the bottom border of the header row. The pointer changes to ÷.

2. Press and hold down the **Alt** key and the mouse button. The row heights are displayed in the vertical ruler.

3. While holding down the **Alt** key, drag the pointer down until row 1 is about 1 inch high, and then release the mouse button. Notice that the height of the other rows in the table is not affected by this change.

The EverRipe table now looks much better with its new column width and row height. Next you'll align the text to make the table even more attractive.

Aligning Text Within Cells

Aligning the text within the cells of a table makes the information easier to read. For example, aligning a column of numbers or percentages along the right margin helps the reader to quickly compare the values. At the same time, centering a row of headings makes a table more visually appealing. You can align text within the active cell the same way you do other text—with the alignment buttons on the Formatting toolbar. However, the alignment buttons on the Tables and Borders toolbar provide more options.

The percentage and dollar amounts in columns C and D would be much easier to read if you were to align the numbers on the right side of the cells. In the process of right-aligning the numbers, you can also right-align the word "Total" in the merged cell at the bottom of columns A, B, and C. The table also would look better with the headings centered. You'll begin by selecting and formatting all of columns C and D.

To right-align the numerical data and center the headings:

1. Move the pointer to the top of column C until the pointer changes to ↓, and then click the top of the column to select the entire column (including the merged cell at the bottom of the column.)

2. Drag the pointer to the right to select column D as well. Now that you've selected the columns, you can align the text within them.

3. Click the **Align Right** button on the Formatting toolbar. The numbers line up along the right edges of the cells. In addition, the word "Total" in the merged cell aligns next to the bottom cell in the Initial Cost column.

   TROUBLE? If more than just the numbers, column headings, and Total cell are right-aligned within the table, you may have selected the wrong block of cells. Click the Undo button on the Standard toolbar, and then repeat Steps 1 through 3.

   Notice that in the process of formatting Columns C and D, you right-aligned two of the headings ("Percent of Total Cost" and "Initial Cost"). You will reformat those headings in the next step, when you center the text in row 1 both horizontally and vertically in each cell.

4. Click the selection bar next to row 1. All of row 1 is selected.

5. Click the **Align** list arrow on the Tables and Borders toolbar to display a palette of nine alignment options.

6. Click the **Align Center** button in the middle of the palette. The text becomes centered both horizontally and vertically in the row.

7. Click anywhere in the table to deselect the row. See Figure 3-27.

Figure 3-27	TABLE WITH NEWLY ALIGNED TEXT

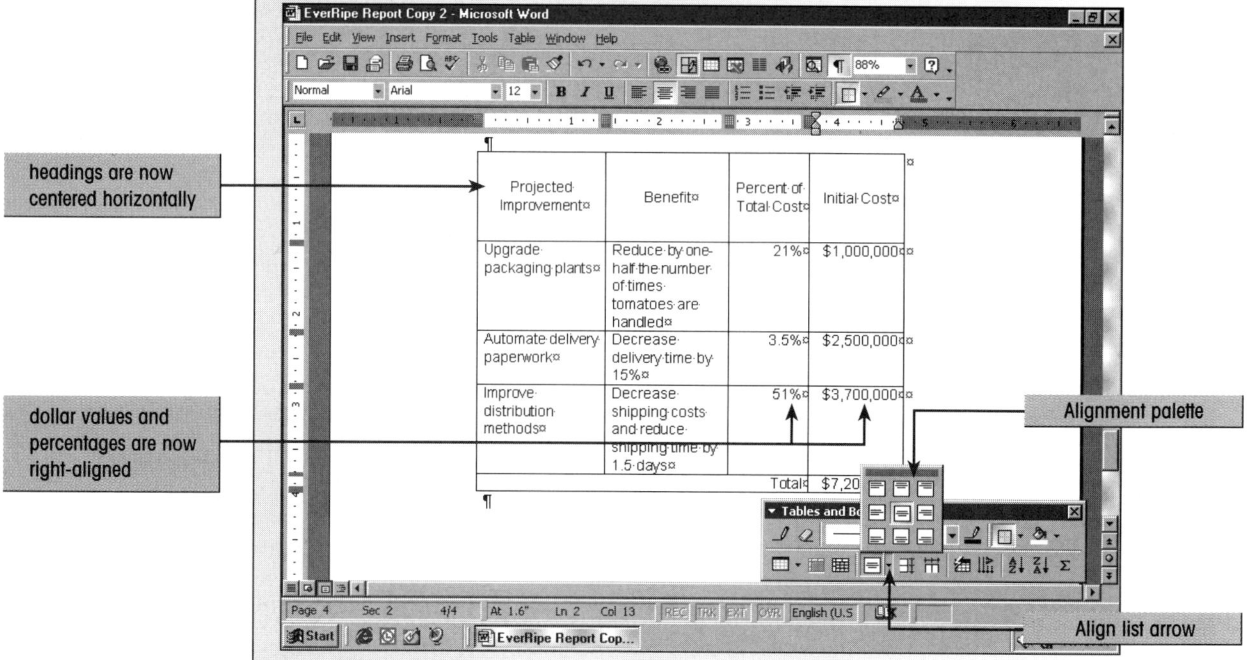

headings are now centered horizontally

dollar values and percentages are now right-aligned

Alignment palette

Align list arrow

TROUBLE? If more than just the heading row is centered, click the Undo button on the Standard toolbar, and then repeat Steps 4 through 7.

8. Save the document with the current changes.

The tables look better with the headings centered and the numbers right-aligned. You now decide to make the table more attractive and easier to read by changing the table's borders and rules.

Changing Borders

It's important to keep in mind the distinction between gridlines and borders. Gridlines are light gray lines that indicate the structure of the table on the screen and that do not show up on the printed page. Borders are darker lines overlaying the gridlines, which do appear on the printed page. When you create a table using the Insert Table button, Word automatically applies a thin black border, so you can't actually see the underlying gridlines.

After you have created a table, you can add new borders, erase existing borders, or modify existing borders by changing their line weights and line styles. **Line weight** refers to the thickness of the border. You can use any combination of these formats you like.

To modify the table's existing borders:

1. Verify that the insertion point is located within the table.

2. Click the **Line Weight** list arrow on the Tables and Borders toolbar, and then click **2¼ pt**.

TROUBLE? If the Office Assistant opens, click the Cancel button to close it. Then continue with Step 3.

3. Move the Draw Table pointer ✏ to the upper-left corner of the table, and then click the top of each cell in row 1. The top border becomes a thicker line.

4. Repeat Step 3 to draw a thicker line below the header row, above the Totals row, and at the bottom of the table. If you make a mistake, click the Undo button 🔄 on the Standard toolbar to reverse it.

Now you'll use a similar method to remove borders (without removing the underlying gridlines) between rows of the table.

5. Click the **Line Style** list arrow on the Tables and Borders toolbar, and then click **No Border**.

6. Click the bottom of each cell in row 2. Only the light gray gridline remains between the first two rows of data.

TROUBLE? If you don't see the light gray gridline, click Table on the menu bar and then click Show Gridlines.

7. Repeat Step 6 to remove the horizontal line below row 3.

8. Press the **Esc** key to turn off the Draw Table pointer. See Figure 3-28.

Figure 3-28	TABLE AFTER CHANGING LINE WEIGHTS AND STYLES

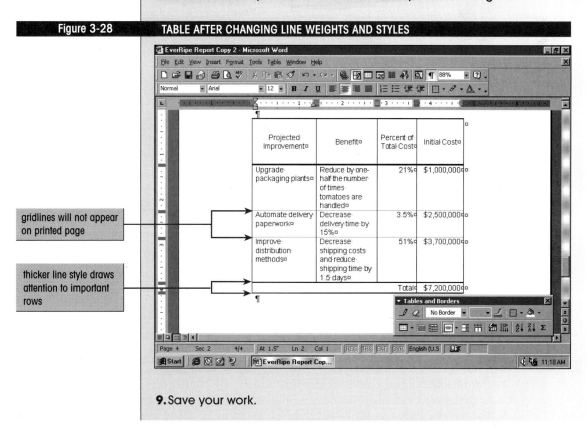

gridlines will not appear on printed page

thicker line style draws attention to important rows

9. Save your work.

Changing the borders has made the table more attractive. You finish formatting the table by adding shading to the cells containing the headings.

Adding Shading

With the Borders and Shading dialog box, adding **shading** (a gray or colored background) to text is a simple task. Shading is especially useful in tables when you want to emphasize headings, totals, or other important items. In most cases, when you add shading to a table, you also need to bold format the shaded text to make it easier to read.

You now will add a light gray shading to the heading row and format the headings in bold.

To add shading to the heading row and change the headings to bold:

1. Click the selection bar to the left of row 1 to select the heading row of the table.

2. Click the **Shading Color** list arrow on the Tables and Borders toolbar. A palette of shading options opens.

3. Point to the fifth gray square from the left, in the top row. The ScreenTip "Gray-15%" appears. See Figure 3-29.

Figure 3-29 **SHADING OPTIONS**

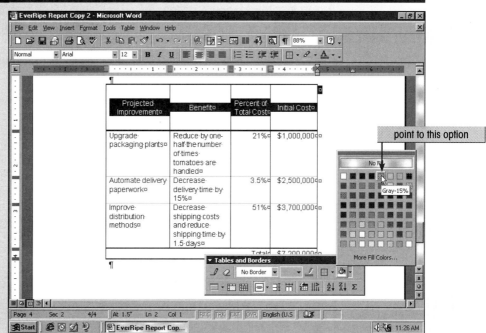

4. Click the **Gray-15%** square. A light gray background appears in the heading row. Now you need to format the text in bold to make the headings stand out from the shading.

5. Click the **Bold** button **B** on the Formatting toolbar to make the headings bold.

   TROUBLE? If any of the headings break incorrectly (for example, if the "t" in "Cost" moves to the next line), you might need to widen columns to accommodate the bold letters. Drag the column borders as necessary to adjust the column widths so that all the column headings are displayed correctly.

6. Click in the selection bar next to the last row to select the Total row.

7. Click **B**. The Total row now appears in bold.

8. Click anywhere outside the Total row to deselect it. Your table should look like Figure 3-30.

Figure 3-30 — FORMATTED HEADING AND TOTAL ROWS

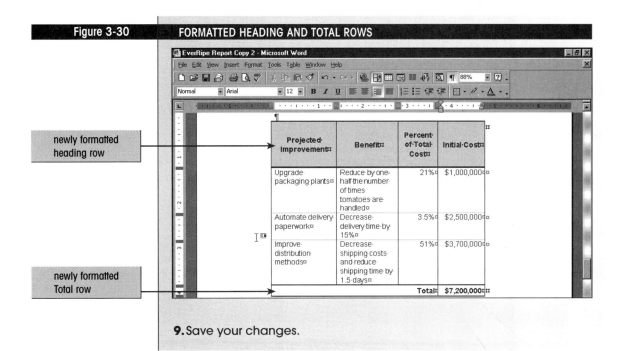

newly formatted heading row

newly formatted Total row

9. Save your changes.

Rotating Text in a Cell

Brittany stops by to take a look at the table so far. She mentions that it is possible to rotate text within the cells of a table. You decide to try rotating the headings to a vertical position to see how they look.

To rotate the headings vertically:

1. Select the heading row.

2. Click the **Change Text Direction** button in the Tables and Borders toolbar, and then click anywhere in the table to deselect the heading row. The table headings are now formatted vertically in their cells, as shown in Figure 3-31.

Figure 3-31 — ROTATED TEXT

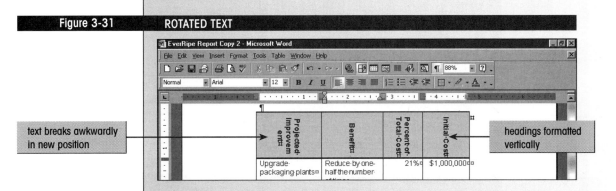

text breaks awkwardly in new position

headings formatted vertically

Notice that the "Project Improvement" heading now breaks awkwardly. You could widen the first row to improve its appearance. But after reviewing the rotated headings, you decide you like them better formatted horizontally. You'll return them to their original position by using the Change Text Direction button again.

3. Select the heading row, and then click ⌷ again. The headings are still format-ted vertically, but now the text flows from bottom to top.

4. Click ⌷ again. The headings are now formatted horizontally. Because you are finished with the Tables and Borders toolbar, you will close it.

5. Click the **Close** button ⌧ on the Tables and Borders toolbar to close the toolbar.

You will finish formatting your table by centering it on the page.

Centering a Table

If a table doesn't fill the entire page width, you can center it between the left and right margins. The Center button on the Formatting toolbar centers only text within each selected cell. It does not center the entire table across the page. To center a table across the page (between the left and right margins), you use the Table Properties command.

The EverRipe table will stand out more and look better if it is centered between the left and right margins.

To center the table across the page:

1. Click anywhere in the table, click **Table** on the menu bar, and then click **Table Properties**. The Table Properties dialog box opens.

2. Click the **Table** tab if necessary.

3. In the Alignment section click the **Center** option. See Figure 3-32.

Figure 3-32   TABLE TAB OF THE TABLE PROPERTIES DIALOG BOX

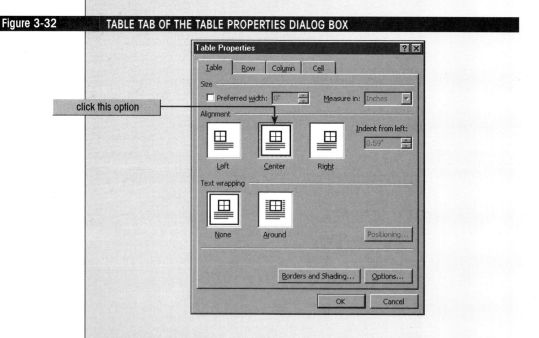

click this option

4. Click the **OK** button. The table centers between the left and right margins.

5. Save the document as **EverRipe Report Final Copy**.

Now that you're finished with the EverRipe table, you want to print a copy of the full report for Brittany. You'll preview the report first to make sure the table fits on the fourth page.

To preview the table:

1. Click the **Print Preview** button on the Standard toolbar to open the Print Preview window.

2. Scroll to view all the pages of the report.

3. Click the **Print** button on the Print Preview toolbar to print the report, then close the document and exit Word.

You now have a hardcopy of the EverRipe report including the table, which summarizes the report text. Your four-page finished report should look like Figure 3-33.

Figure 3-33   **FINISHED EVERRIPE REPORT**

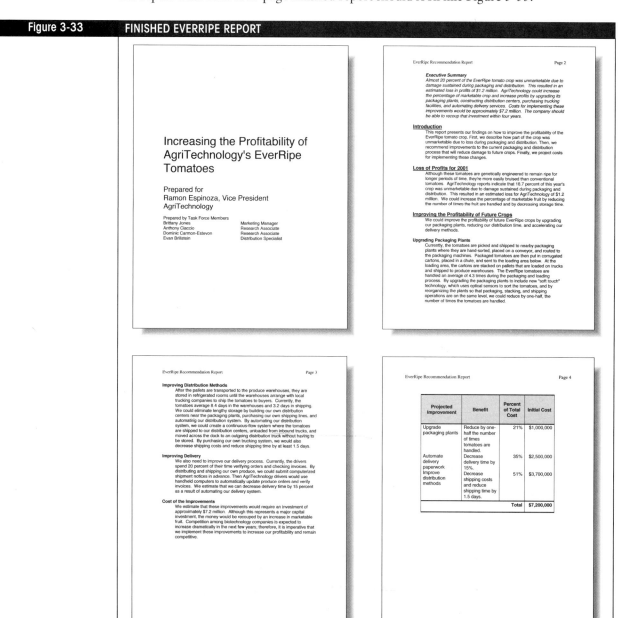

In this tutorial, you have planned and formatted Brittany's recommendation report and added a table to summarize the report recommendations. As a result, the report information is readily available to readers who want to skim for the most important points, as well as to those who want more detailed information.

Session 3.2 QUICK CHECK

1. How do you adjust the width of the columns in a table?

2. Why would you usually right-align numbers in a table?

3. Define the following terms in your own words:

   a. merge
   b. rotate
   c. border
   d. shading

4. Explain how to add a row to the bottom of a table.

5. Explain how to total a column of numbers in a table.

6. In what order would the following numbers appear in a table if you sorted them in ascending numerical order: 25, 10, 75, 45?

7. How do you center a table between the left and right margins?

REVIEW ASSIGNMENTS

AgriTechnology adopted the recommendations the task force made in the EverRipe report. It is now two years later and the task force is issuing a report on the progress of the new packaging, distribution, and delivery policies. You'll format this report now.

1. If necessary, start Word and make sure your Data Disk is in the appropriate disk drive, and check your screen to make sure your settings match those in the tutorial. Display nonprinting characters as necessary.

2. Open the file **StatRep** from the Review folder for Tutorial 3 on your Data Disk, and then save it as **AgTech Status Report**.

3. Select the list of task force members and their titles, and then insert a left tab stop 2.5 inches from the left margin.

4. Click after the "t" in "Distribution Specialist," press the Enter key, and then type your name. Press the Tab key to move the insertion point to the tab stop, and then type a title for yourself.

5. Divide the document into two sections. Insert a section break so that the executive summary begins on a new page.

Explore   6. Vertically align the first section of the document using the Justified alignment option in the Page Setup dialog box, and view the results in Print Preview.

Explore

7. Add a footer to section 2. Click View on the menu bar, and then click Header and Footer. Use the Word online Help system to learn the functions of the buttons on the Header and Footer toolbar. Then, on the Header and Footer toolbar, click the Switch Between Header and Footer button to move to the footer area of section 2. Click the Same as Previous button to deselect it. Using the same techniques you used to create a header in the tutorial, create a footer for section 2 that reads "EverRipe Status Report" at the left margin. Insert the current date at the right margin. (*Hint:* Use the Insert Date button on the Header and Footer toolbar to insert the date.) Use the Formatting toolbar to format the footer and date in 9-point bold Arial.

Explore

8. Create a header for section 2 that aligns your name at the left margin and centers the page number preceded by the word "Page." Don't forget to deselect the Same as Previous button. (*Hint:* To center the page number, use the second tab stop.) Click Close on the Header and Footer toolbar.

9. Save, preview, and print the document; then close it.

Open the file **ZonReq** from the Review folder for Tutorial 3 on your Data Disk, save the document as **Zoning Request**, and then complete the following:

10. On the first page, replace "Your Name" with your first and last name.

11. Under the heading "Benefits to the Community," select the three lines of text containing tabs. Insert a left tab stop 3 inches from the left margin.

12. Divide the document into two sections. Begin the second section with the introduction on a new page.

13. Use the Ctrl+Enter key combination to insert a page break before the line "The new jobs would be divided as follows:".

14. Vertically align the first section of the document using the Center alignment option in the Page Setup dialog box.

15. Create a header for section 2 that prints "Zoning Request" at the left margin and has a right-aligned page number preceded by the word "Page." (*Hint*: Deselect the Same as Previous button on the Header and Footer toolbar.)

16. On the Header and Footer toolbar, click the Switch Between Header and Footer button to move to the footer area of section 2. Using the same techniques you used to create a header in the tutorial, create a footer for section 2 that aligns your name at the left margin and the date on the right margin.

17. Click the Close button on the Header and Footer toolbar, then review the new headers and footers in print layout view.

Explore

18. Modify the page number in the header so that it indicates the total number of pages in the document. Click View on the menu bar, click Header and Footer, click to the right of the page number, press the spacebar, type "of" (without the quotation marks), press the spacebar, and then click the Insert Number of Pages button on the Header and Footer toolbar.

19. Save the document.

20. Insert a page break at the end of the document.

21. Insert a table consisting of four rows and three columns.

22. Type the headings "Project," "Cost," and "Jobs Added" in row 1.

23. In row 2, type "Expand Packaging Plant," "$1,200,000," and "175" in the appropriate cells.

24. In row 3, type "Miscellaneous Items," "$200,000," and "2" in the appropriate cells.

25. In row 4, type "Build Distribution Center," "$1,300,000," and "125" in the appropriate cells.

26. Sort the table in ascending numerical order, by the Jobs Added column.

27. Select the entire Project column, click Table on the menu bar, point to Insert, and then click Columns to the Right to insert a new column between the Project column and the Cost column. Type the heading "Priority" in the new cell B1, press the down arrow, type 3, press the down arrow, type 2, press the down arrow, and then type 1.

28. Add a new row to the bottom of the table. Type "Total" in the new cell A5, at the bottom of the Project column.

29. Merge the "Total" cell with the cell to its right. Align the word "Total" on the right of the newly merged cell.

30. Use the AutoSum button on the Tables and Borders toolbar to total the Cost and Jobs Added columns. Click the Cost total to select it, and then format it without decimal points using the Formula command on the Table menu. Notice that the Total of the Cost column is $2,700,000, and the total of the Jobs Added column is 302.

31. Delete the Miscellaneous Items row.

Explore   32. Update both AutoSum formulas to reflect the deleted row. To update a formula, select the cell containing the formula, and then press the F9 key. The totals are updated to include only the rows currently in the table. The total of the Cost column should now be $2,500,000. The total of the Jobs Added column should now be 300.

33. Center the table on the page.

34. Drag the right border of column C (the Cost column) to the left until the column is about 0.8 inches wide. Drag the right border of column D (the Jobs Added column) to the left until the column is about 0.9 inches wide.

Explore   35. Switch to print layout view, if necessary, and then use the Table move handle to select the entire table, and then format the text as 14-point Times New Roman.

Explore   36. Try adjusting the column widths to accommodate the newly formatted text by double-clicking the borders between columns. First click anywhere within the table to deselect any selected text or cells. Double-click the border between columns A and B. The width of column A adjusts automatically to accommodate the longest entry. Adjust the widths of the other columns by clicking on their right borders.

37. Right-align the numbers in the table. The "Total" label should also be right-aligned.

38. Format the heading row by adding a light gray shading. Format the headings in bold as well.

39. Use the Line Weight list arrow on the Tables and Borders toolbar to add a 2¼-point border around the outside of the table. Also, change the border above the Total row to 2¼ point. Instead of clicking the borders you want to change, try drawing with the pointer. If you don't drag the pointer far enough, the Office Assistant may appear to offer some advice. Read the information it provides and click OK. To turn off the Draw Tables pointer, press the Esc key.

40. Increase the height of the heading row to approximately 0.8 inches. Center the headings vertically and horizontally using the Align Center option on the Tables and Borders toolbar.

41. Save, preview, print, and close the document.

Word will convert text separated by commas, paragraph marks, or tabs into a table. To try this feature, open the file **Members** from the Review folder for Tutorial 3 on your Data Disk, and save it as **Zoning Board Members**. Then complete the following:

42. Select the list of zoning board members (including the heading), click Table on the menu bar, and point to Convert, and then click Text to Table. In the Convert Text to Table dialog box, make sure the settings indicate that the table should have two columns and that the text is separated by commas. Then click the OK button. Word converts the list of task force members into a table.

43. Click cell B5, in the lower-right corner of the table, and then press the Tab key. Type your own name in the new cell A6, press the Tab key, and then type "Ward 2" in cell B6.

44. Format the table appropriately using the techniques you learned in the tutorial. Be sure to adjust the column widths to close up any extra space.

Explore   45. Place the pointer over the Table resize handle, just outside the lower-right corner of the table. Drag the double-arrow pointer to increase the size of the height and width of each cell. Notice that all the parts of the table increase proportionally. Click the Undo button to return the table to its original format.

46. Save the document; then preview and print it.

CASE PROBLEMS

Case 1. Ocean Breeze Bookstore Annual Report   As manager of Ocean Breeze Bookstore in San Diego, California, you must submit an annual report to the Board of Directors.

1. If necessary, start Word, make sure your Data Disk is in the appropriate drive, and check your screen to make sure your settings match those in the tutorials.

2. Open the file **OceanRep** from the Cases folder for Tutorial 3 on your Data Disk, and save it as **Ocean Breeze Report**.

3. Divide the document into two sections. Begin section 2 with the introduction on a new page.

4. Format the title ("Annual Report") and the subtitle ("Ocean Breeze Bookstore") using the font and font size of your choice. Vertically align the first section using the alignment option of your choice.

Explore   5. Move the insertion point to section 2. Create a header for the entire document that aligns "Ocean Breeze Annual Report" on the left margin, your name in the center, and the current date on the right margin. Click the Show Previous button on the Header and Footer toolbar to view the header text for section 1.

6. Select the list of members under the heading "Board of Directors." Insert a left tab stop 4.5 inches from the left margin.

7. Preview and save the document.

8. Insert a page break at the end of the document.

9. Insert a table consisting of four rows and three columns.

10. Insert the headings "Name," "Title," and "Duties." Fill in the rows with the relevant information about the store personnel, which you will find listed in the report. Add new rows as needed.

11. Adjust the table column widths so the information is presented attractively.

12. Increase the height of the heading row, center the column headings horizontally and vertically, and then bold them.

Explore 13. Use Help to learn how to insert a row within a table. Insert a row in the middle of the table, and add your name to the list of store managers. Readjust the column widths as needed.

14. Format the heading row with a light gray shading of your choice.

15. Change the outside border of the table to 2¼-point line weight.

16. Save, preview, print, and close the document.

Case 2. Ultimate Travel's "Europe on a Budget" Report   As director of Ultimate Travel's "Europe on a Budget" tour, you need to write a report summarizing this year's tour.

1. If necessary, start Word, make sure your Data Disk is in the appropriate drive, and check your screen to make sure your settings match those in the tutorials.

2. Open the file **Europe** from the Cases folder for Tutorial 3 on your Data Disk, and save it as **Europe Tour Report**.

3. Replace "Your Name" in the first page with your first and last name.

4. Divide the document into two sections. Begin the second section on a new page, with the summary that starts "This report summarizes and evaluates...."

5. Vertically align the first section using the Center alignment option.

6. Create a header for section 2 that contains the centered text "Ultimate Travel." (*Hint:* To center text in the header, use the second tab stop. Deselect the Same as Previous button before you begin.)

7. On the Header and Footer toolbar, click the Switch Between Header and Footer button to move to the footer area of the document. Using the same techniques you used to create a header in the tutorial, create a footer for section 2 that aligns "Evaluation Report" on the left margin and the date on the right margin. (*Hint:* Deselect the Same as Previous button first.)

8. In the table, bold the text in column A (the left column), and then rotate it so that text is formatted vertically, from bottom to top.

9. Adjust the row and column widths as necessary.

10. Delete the blank row 2.

11. Format column A with a light gray shading.

12. Change the border around column A to 2¼-point line weight.

13. Save, preview, print, and close the document.

Case 3. Classical CD Sales at The Master's Touch   Austin Cornelius is the purchasing agent for The Master's Touch, a music store in Little Rock, Arkansas. Each month, Austin publishes a list of the classical CDs that are on sale at The Master's Touch. He has asked you to create a table showing this month's list of sale items.

1. Open the file **Classics** from the Cases folder for Tutorial 3 on your Data Disk, and save it as **Classical Music CDs**.

Explore

2. Highlight the list of CDs—Chopin Nocturnes through The Nine Symphonies—separated by commas, and convert it into a table. (*Hint:* Click Table on the menu bar, point to Convert, and then click Text to Table. In the dialog box, select Commas as the Separate text at option. Make sure the Number of columns is set to 5.)

Explore

3. Insert an additional row for headings by selecting the top row of the table, and then clicking the Insert Rows button in the Standard toolbar.

4. Type the following headings (in a sans serif boldface font) in this order: "Title," "Artist," "Label," "Number of CDs in Set," and "Price."

5. Insert a row below "The Best of Chopin," and then type the following in the cells: "Beethoven Piano Sonatas," "Alfred Brendel," "Vox," "2," "18.95."

6. Open the Tables and Borders toolbar if necessary, and then sort the rows in the table in ascending alphabetical order by title.

7. Center the numbers in the "Number of CDs in Set" column.

Explore

8. Split cells to allow for two columns of pricing information. Select the cells containing prices (cells E2 through E10), and then click the Split Cells button on the Tables and Borders toolbar. In the Split Cells dialog box, deselect the "Merge cells before split" check box. (If you keep this option selected, Word moves all the prices into one cell before splitting each of the cells into two.) Verify that the Number of columns setting is 2, so that Word will divide each cell into two cells (or columns). Click OK.

Explore

9. Click the Line Weight list arrow on the Tables and Borders toolbar, click 1½ pt, and then use the Draw Table pointer to draw a horizontal line in cell E1 directly below the word "Price." Next, use the Split Cells button again to divide the new, empty cell below the "Price" cell into two. In the new, empty cell on the left (directly above the column of prices), type "CD Club Members." In the new, blank cell on the right (directly above the blank column), type "Non-Members." For each title, enter a Non-Members' price that is $1.00 more than the CD Club Members price.

10. Adjust column widths as necessary.

11. Add 2¼-point horizontal borders to make the table easier to read.

12. Save your document; then preview, print, and close it.

Case 4. Computer Training at Pottery Row, Inc.   Joseph Keats is the director of the Human Resources department at Pottery Row, Inc., a mail-order firm specializing in home furnishings. He has contracted with Bright Star Learning systems for a series of in-house training seminars on intermediate and advanced word processing skills. He asks you to create an informational flier for posting on bulletin boards around the office. Among other things, the flier should include Bright Star Learning Systems' corporate logo (an orange, five-pointed star). You begin by drawing a sketch, similar to the one shown in Figure 3-34. You decide to take advantage of the Word table features to structure the information in the flier.

Figure 3-34   SKETCH FOR BRIGHT STAR FLIER

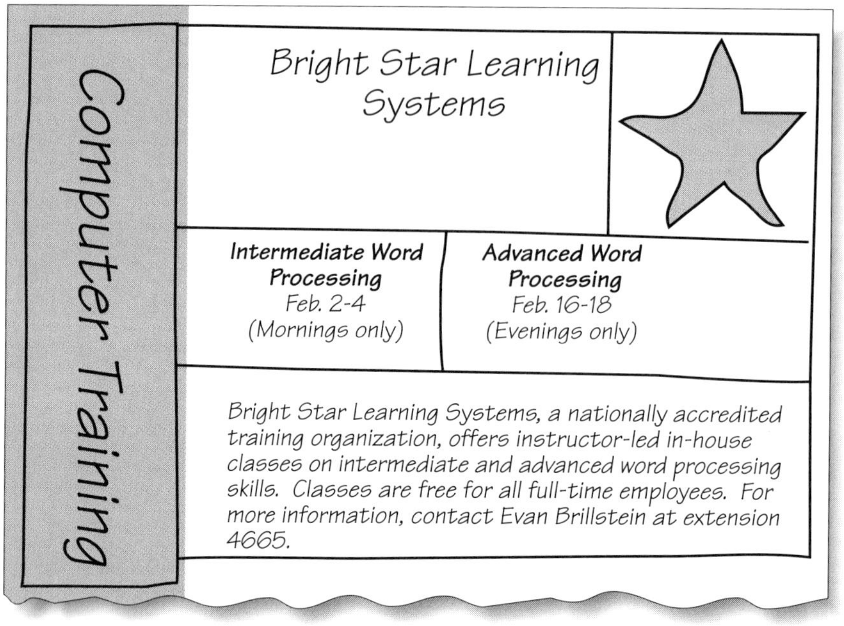

1. Open a new, blank document and save it as **Bright Star Training** in the Cases folder for Tutorial 3.

2. If necessary, switch to print layout view and display the Tables and Borders toolbar.

Explore

3. Click the Draw Table button on the Tables and Borders toolbar, if necessary, to select the button and change the pointer to a pencil shape. Click in the upper-left corner of the document (near the paragraph mark), and drag down and to the right to draw a rectangle about 6 inches wide and 3.5 inches high.

Explore

4. Continue to use the Draw Table pointer to draw the columns and rows shown in Figure 3-34. For example, to draw the column border for the "Computer Training" column, click at the top of the rectangle, where you want the column to begin, and drag down to the bottom of the rectangle. Use the same technique to draw rows. If you make a mistake, use the Undo button. To delete a border, click the Eraser button in the Tables and Borders toolbar, click the border you want to erase, and then click the Eraser button again to turn it off. Keep in mind that you can also merge cells, if necessary. Don't expect to draw the table perfectly the first time. You may have to practice a while until you become comfortable with the Draw Table pointer, but once you can use it well, you will find it a helpful tool for creating complex tables.

5. In the left column, type the text "Computer Training," rotate the text to position it vertically in the table, and format the text in 26-point Times New Roman, so that it fills the height of the column. If the text does not fit in one row, drag the table border down until it does. (*Hint:* You will probably have to adjust and readjust the row and column borders throughout this project, until all the elements of the table are positioned properly.)

6. Type the remaining text, as shown in Figure 3-34. Replace the name "Evan Brillstein" with your own name. Use bold and italic as necessary to draw attention to key elements. Use the font styles, font sizes, and alignment options you think appropriate.

Explore 7. Click the Drawing button on the Standard toolbar to display the Drawing toolbar. Now you can insert the Bright Star corporate logo in the upper-right cell, using one of the tools on the Drawing toolbar. Click the AutoShapes button on the Drawing toolbar, point to Stars and Banners, and then click the 5-Point Star. Move the cross-hair pointer over the upper-right cell, then click and drag to draw a star that fits roughly within the cell borders. After you draw the star, it remains selected, as indicated by the square boxes, called selection handles, that surround it. Click the lower-right selection handle, and drag up or down to adjust the size of the star so that it fits within the cell borders more precisely. With the star still selected, click the Fill Color list arrow on the Drawing toolbar, and then click a gold color in the color palette.

8. Use the Shading Color button on the Tables and Borders toolbar to add the same color background to the "Computer Training" column.

9. Adjust column widths and row heights so that the table is attractive and easy-to-read.

Explore 10. Now that you have organized the information using the Word table tools, you can remove the borders so that the printed flier doesn't look like a table. Click the Table move handle to select the entire table, click Table on the menu bar, click Table Properties, click the Table tab, click the Borders and Shading button, and then click the Borders tab, click the None option, click the OK button, and then click the OK button again. The borders are removed from the flier, leaving only the underlying gridlines, which will not appear on the printed page.

11. Save your work, preview the flier, make any necessary adjustments, print it, and then close the document.

INTERNET ASSIGNMENTS

The purpose of the Internet Assignments is to challenge you to find information on the Internet that you can use to create effective documents. The actual assignments are updated and maintained on the Course Technology Web site. Log on to the Internet and use your Web browser to go to the Student Online Companion to accompany this text at **www.course.com/NewPerspectives/office2000**. Click the Word link, and then click the link for Tutorial 3.

QUICK CHECK ANSWERS

Session 3.1

1. **a.** The location where text moves when you press the Tab key.

   b. The intersection of a row and a column in a table.

   c. Information arranged in horizontal rows and vertical columns.

   d. A tab stop that aligns numerical data on the decimal point.

   e. A unit or part of a document that can have its own page orientation, margins, headers, footers, and vertical alignment.

2. Insert a section break, move the insertion point within the section you want to align, click File, click Page Setup, click the Layout tab, select Center in the Vertical alignment list box, make sure This section is selected in the Apply to list box, and then click OK.

3. A header appears at the top of a page, whereas a footer appears at the bottom of a page.

4. Move the insertion point to the location where you want the table to appear. Click the Insert Table button on the Standard toolbar. In the grid, click and drag to select four columns and six rows, and then release the mouse button

5. If the insertion point is in the rightmost cell in a row, press the Tab key. Otherwise, press the ↓ key.

6. Click View on the menu bar, click Header and Footer, verify that the insertion point is located in the Header area, press Tab to move the insertion point to where you want the page number to appear, and then click the Insert Page Number button on the Header and Footer toolbar.

7. Select the text whose tab alignment you want to change, click the tab alignment selector on the far left of the horizontal ruler until the appropriate tab stop alignment style appears, and then click in the horizontal ruler where you want to set the new tab stop.

8. You might want to divide a document into sections if you wanted to center part of the document between the top and bottom margins.

9. It's better to use a table rather than tab stops when you need to organize a lot of complicated information.

10. Click the Table move handle.

Session 3.2

1. Drag the right border of each column to a new position.

2. Right-aligning numbers in a table makes the numbers easier to read.

3. **a.** Combine two or more cells into one.

   b. Move text in a cell so that it is formatted vertically rather than horizontally.

   c. The outline of a row, cell, column, or table.

   d. A gray or colored background used to highlight parts of a table.

4. Click the rightmost cell in the bottom row of the table, and then press the Tab key.

5. Click the cell where you want the total to appear, click the AutoSum button on the Tables and Borders toolbar, click the total to select it, click Table on the menu bar, click Formula, select the number format you want, and then click OK.

6. 10, 25, 45, 75

7. Click anywhere in the table, click Table on the menu bar, click Table Properties, click the Table tab, click Center, and then click OK.

In this tutorial you will:

- Identify desktop-publishing features

- Create a title with WordArt

- Create newspaper-style columns

- Insert clip art

- Wrap text around a graphic

- Incorporate drop caps

- Use symbols and special typographic characters

- Add a page border

DESKTOP PUBLISHING A NEWSLETTER

Creating a Newsletter for FastFad Manufacturing Company

CASE

FastFad Manufacturing Company

Gerrit Polansky works for FastFad Manufacturing Company, which designs and manufactures plastic figures (action figures, vehicles, and other toys) for promotional sales and giveaways in the fast-food and cereal industries. Gerrit keeps FastFad's sales staff informed about new products by producing and distributing a monthly newsletter that briefly describes these new items and gives ideas for marketing them. Recently, FastFad added MiniMovers—small plastic cars, trucks, and other vehicles—to its line of plastic toys. Gerrit needs to get the information about these products to the sales staff quickly so that the company can market the toys to FastFad's clients while the toys are still popular. He has asked you to help him create the newsletter.

The newsletter must be eye-catching because the quantity of printed product material sales reps get makes it difficult for them to focus on any one product. Gerrit also wants you to create a newsletter that is neat, organized, and professional-looking. He would like it to contain headings (so the sales reps can scan it quickly for the major points) as well as graphics that will give the newsletter a memorable "look." He wants you to include a picture that will reinforce the newsletter content and distinguish the product.

In this tutorial, you'll plan the layout of the newsletter, keeping in mind the audience (the sales representatives). Then you'll get acquainted with the desktop-publishing features and elements you'll need to use to create the newsletter. Also, you'll learn how desktop publishing differs from other word-processing tasks. You'll format the title using an eye-catching design and divide the document into newspaper-style columns to make it easier for the sales reps to read. To add interest and focus to the text, you'll include a piece of pre-designed art. You'll then fine-tune the newsletter layout, give it a more professional appearance with typographic characters, and put a border around the page to give the newsletter a finished look.

SESSION 4.1

In this session you will see how Gerrit planned his newsletter and learn about desktop-publishing features and elements. Then you will create the newsletter title using WordArt, modify the title's appearance, and format the text of the newsletter into news-paper-style columns.

Planning the Document

The newsletter will provide a brief overview of the new FastFad products, followed by a short explanation of what the MiniMovers are and why children will like them. Like most newsletters, it will be written in an informal style that conveys information quickly. The newsletter title will be eye-catching and will help readers quickly identify the document. Newsletter text will be split into two columns to make it easier to read, and headings will help readers scan the information quickly. A picture will add interest and illustrate the newsletter content. Drop caps and other desktop-publishing elements will help draw readers' attention to certain information and make the newsletter design attractive and professional.

Elements of Desktop Publishing

Desktop publishing is the production of commercial-quality printed material using a desktop computer system from which you can enter and edit text, create graphics, compose or lay out pages, and print documents. The following elements are commonly associated with desktop publishing:

- **High-quality printing**. A laser printer or high-resolution inkjet printer produces final output.
- **Multiple fonts.** Two or three font types and sizes provide visual interest, guide the reader through the text, and convey the tone of the document.
- **Graphics.** Graphics, such as horizontal or vertical lines (called **rules**), boxes, electronic art, and digitized photographs help illustrate a concept or product, draw a reader's attention to the document, and make the text visually appealing.
- **Typographic characters**. Typographic characters such as typographic long dashes, called **em dashes** (—), in place of double hyphens (--), separate dependent clauses; typographic medium-width dashes, called en dashes (–), are used in place of hyphens (-) as minus signs and in ranges of numbers; and typographic bullets (•) signal items in a list.
- **Columns and other formatting features.** Columns of text, **pull quotes** (small portions of text pulled out of the main text and enlarged), page borders, and other special formatting features that you don't frequently see in letters and other documents distinguish desktop-published documents.

You'll incorporate many of these desktop-publishing elements into the FastFad newsletter for Gerrit.

Word's Desktop-Publishing Features

Successful desktop publishing requires that you first know what elements professionals use to desktop publish a document. Figure 4-1 defines some of the desktop-publishing features included in Word. Gerrit wants you to use these features to produce the final newsletter shown in Figure 4-2. The newsletter includes some of the typical desktop-publishing elements that you can add to a document using Word.

Figure 4-1	WORD DESKTOP PUBLISHING FEATURES

ELEMENT	DESCRIPTION
Columns	Two or more vertical blocks of text that fit on one page
WordArt	Text modified with special effects, such as rotated, curved, bent, shadowed, or shaded letters
Clip art	Prepared graphic images that are ready to be inserted into a document
Drop cap	Oversized first letter of word beginning a paragraph that extends vertically into two or more lines of the paragraph
Typographical symbols	Special characters that are not part of the standard keyboard, such as em dashes (—), copyright symbols (©), or curly quotation marks (")

Figure 4-2	FASTFAD NEWSLETTER

FastFad Update

Announcing FastFad's New Line of Plastic Toys

Remember GI Joe and the Power Rangers? They've come and gone. And Transformers and Match Box cars? They're a thing of the past. But the next craze sure to sweep the country is MiniMovers®.

What Are MiniMovers?

MiniMovers are bright, colorful plastic models with parts that move. With just a push, these pint-size vehicles scoot across the floor; the wheels spin, the propellers turn, and the horns honk. MiniMovers are perfectly sized for pretend play, and they're stylish too.

Why Will Kids Love Them?

These child-size models encourage imaginativeness and play. Made of nearly indestructible plastic, MiniMovers help kids get serious about having fun! We used real experts, kids, as our official toy testers. And based on their play-packed screening, these toys will be the hot new items this year.

Mini Size, Mighty Fun!

MiniMovers let kids visit great places without ever leaving home.

Here's the rundown on our figures:

- Farm set—kids will love the horns on the truck, tractor, and old jalopy.
- Recreation set—ride in style with the beach patrol jeep, dune buggy, and three-wheeler.
- Transportation set—the propellers actually turn on our helicopter, plane, and boat.

After the kids have a full set, they can order our CargoCarrier™, a truck with a detachable trailer, which can carry two MiniMovers inside and one on top.

Just Right for Fun Packs

Our new line of MiniMovers are just right for putting in fun packs for kids ages 4 to 10 years.

MiniMovers are safe and tons of fun. They're perfect for the "Happy Meal" generation.

Your first step is to create the newsletter's title.

Using WordArt to Create the Newsletter Title

Gerrit wants the title of the newsletter, "FastFad Update," to be eye-catching and dramatic, as shown in Figure 4-2. **WordArt**, available in Word as well as other Microsoft Office programs, provides great flexibility in designing text with special effects that expresses the image or mood you want to convey in your printed documents. With WordArt, you can apply color and shading, as well as alter the shape and size of the text. You can easily "wrap" the document text around WordArt shapes.

You begin creating a WordArt image by choosing a text design. Then you type in the text you want to enhance and format it.

When you create a WordArt image, Word switches to print layout view because WordArt images are not visible in normal view. Print layout view is the most appropriate view to use when you are desktop publishing with Word because it shows you exactly how the text and graphics fit on the page. The vertical ruler that appears in print layout view helps you position graphical elements more precisely.

REFERENCE WINDOW   **RW**

Creating Special Text Effects Using WordArt
- Click the Drawing button on the Standard toolbar to display the Drawing toolbar.
- Click the Insert WordArt button on the Drawing toolbar.
- Click the style of text you want to insert, and then click the OK button.
- Type the text you want in the Edit WordArt Text dialog box.
- Click the Font and Size list arrows to select the font and font size you want.
- If you want, click the Bold or Italic button, or both.
- Click the OK button.
- With the WordArt selected, drag any handle to reshape and resize it. To keep the text in the same proportions as the original, press and hold down the Shift key while you drag a handle.

To begin, you'll open the file that contains the unformatted text of the newsletter, often called **copy**, and then you'll use WordArt to create the newsletter title.

To create the title of the newsletter using WordArt:

1. Start Word and insert your Data Disk in the appropriate drive. Make sure your screen matches the figures in this tutorial, and display the nonprinting characters so you can see more accurately where to insert text and graphics.

2. Open the file **MiniInfo** from the Tutorial folder for Tutorial 4 on your Data Disk, and then save it as **FastFad Newsletter** in the same folder.

3. With the insertion point at the beginning of the document, click the **Drawing** button 🖉 on the Standard toolbar to display the Drawing toolbar, which appears at the bottom of the screen, if it is not already displayed.

TROUBLE? If the Drawing toolbar is not positioned at the bottom of the document window, drag it there by its title bar. If you do not see the Drawing toolbar anywhere, right-click the Standard toolbar, and then click Drawing on the shortcut menu.

4. Click the **Insert WordArt** button 🔲 on the Drawing toolbar. The WordArt Gallery dialog box opens, displaying the 30 WordArt styles available.

5. Click the WordArt style in the bottom row, the fourth column from the left, as shown in Figure 4-3.

Figure 4-3   **WORDART GALLERY STYLES**

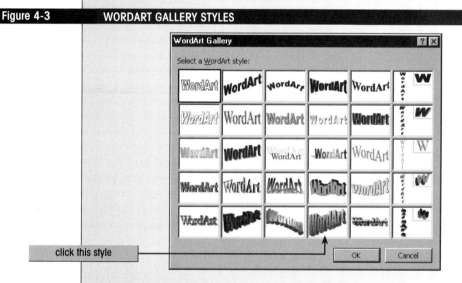

click this style

6. Click the **OK** button. The Edit WordArt Text dialog box opens, displaying the default text "Your Text Here," which you will replace with the newsletter title.

7. Type **FastFad Update**. Make sure you make "FastFad" one word with no space.

8. Click the **OK** button.

The WordArt image appears over the existing text at the top of the newsletter, the WordArt toolbar appears on the screen, and the document changes to print layout view. See Figure 4-4. Don't be concerned that the image partially covers the newsletter text or if it's below the first paragraph. You'll fix that later. Note that the position of the WordArt object relative to the text is indicated by a small anchor symbol in the left margin. If you want to add text before the WordArt object, you need to type the text before the anchor symbol. If you want to add a section break to the document after the WordArt, you need to insert a section break after the anchor symbol.

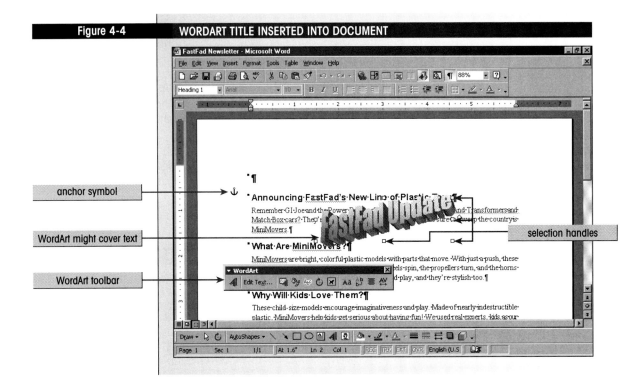

Figure 4-4   **WORDART TITLE INSERTED INTO DOCUMENT**

The WordArt image you have created is considered a Word drawing **object**. This means that you can modify its appearance (color, shape, size, alignment, and so forth) using the buttons on the Drawing toolbar or the WordArt toolbar. Although the object looks like text, Word does not treat it like text. The object is not visible in normal view, and Word will not spell check it as it does regular text. Think of it as a piece of art rather than as text.

The WordArt object is selected, as indicated by the eight small squares, called **resize handles,** surrounding it, and the small yellow diamond called an **adjustment handle**. The resize and adjustment handles let you change the size and shape of the selected object. Before you change the size of the object, you'll first alter its font size and formatting. The default font for this WordArt style is Impact (a sans serif font), but Gerrit wants you to change it to Times New Roman (a serif font) to provide contrast to the sans serif headings in the newsletter.

To change the font and formatting of the WordArt object:

1. Verify that the WordArt object is selected, as indicated by the selection handles.

2. Click the **Edit Text** button on the WordArt toolbar. The Edit WordArt Text dialog box opens.

3. Click the **Font** list arrow, scroll to and then click **Times New Roman**. The text in the preview box changes to Times New Roman.

   TROUBLE? If you do not have Times New Roman available, choose another serif font.

4. Click the **Size** list arrow, scroll to and then click **40**, click the **Bold** button **B** , and then click the **Italic** button *I* . The text in the preview box enlarges to 40-point bold, italic.

5. Click the **OK** button. The newsletter title changes to 40-point, bold, italic Times New Roman.

The default shape of the WordArt style you selected is an upward-slanting shape called Cascade Up. Gerrit wants something a little more symmetrical. In WordArt, you can change the object to any of the WordArt shapes.

To change the shape of the WordArt object:

1. Click the **WordArt Shape** button on the WordArt toolbar. The palette of shapes appears, with the Cascade Up shape selected.

2. Click the **Deflate** shape (fourth row down, second column from the left), as shown in Figure 4-5.

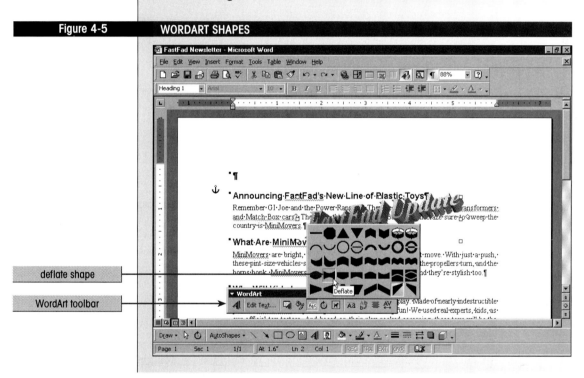

Figure 4-5 | **WORDART SHAPES**

deflate shape

WordArt toolbar

The newsletter title changes to the new WordArt shape.

Editing a WordArt Object

Now that the newsletter title is the font and shape you want, you'll move the title to the top of the newsletter and wrap the newsletter text below the WordArt object. **Text wrapping** is often used in newsletters to prevent text and graphic objects from overlapping, to add interest, and to prevent excessive open areas, called **white space**, from appearing on the page. You can wrap text around objects many different ways in Word. For example, you can have the text wrap above and below the object, through it, or wrap the text to follow the shape of the object, even if the graphic has an irregular shape. The Text Wrapping button on the WordArt or Picture toolbar provides some basic choices, whereas the Layout tab of the Format Picture dialog box provides more advanced options. Because you want a simple wrap, you'll use the Text Wrapping button on the WordArt toolbar.

To insert space between the WordArt object and the newsletter text:

1. With the WordArt object selected, click the **Text Wrapping** button 🔳 on the WordArt toolbar. A menu of text-wrapping options opens. See Figure 4-6.

Figure 4-6 | **TEXT WRAPPING OPTIONS**

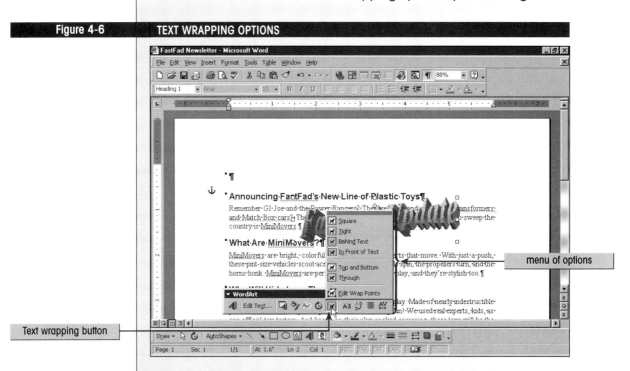

2. Click **Top and Bottom**. The text drops below the newsletter title.

TROUBLE? If the title is not above the text, drag it there now.

Next, you'll position the title and widen it proportionally so it fits neatly within the newsletter margins. You can widen any WordArt object by dragging one of its resize handles. To keep the object the same proportion as the original, you hold down the Shift key as you drag the resize handle. This prevents "stretching" the object more in one direction than the other. After you stretch the WordArt, you'll rotate it slightly so it looks more balanced. Then you'll check the position of its anchor to make sure it is located in a separate paragraph from the text of the newsletter.

To position, enlarge, and rotate the WordArt object:

1. Drag the WordArt object to the left until the lower-left corner of the first "F" in the word "FastFad" is aligned with the left margin and then release the mouse button. Because you can see only the text outline (not the text itself) as you drag the object, you might need to repeat the procedure. Use the left edge of the text or the left margin in the ruler as a guide.

2. With the WordArt object still selected, position the pointer over its lower-right resize handle. The pointer changes to .

3. Press and hold the **Shift** key while you drag the resize handle to the right margin, using the horizontal ruler as a guide. See Figure 4-7. As you drag the handle, the pointer changes to ┼. If necessary, repeat the procedure to make the rightmost edge of the "e" in the word "Update" line up with the right margin. Note that in the process of resizing, the anchor symbol might have moved. You'll fix that later. Now, you'll lower the right side of the WordArt object.

Figure 4-7	RESIZING THE WORDART OBJECT

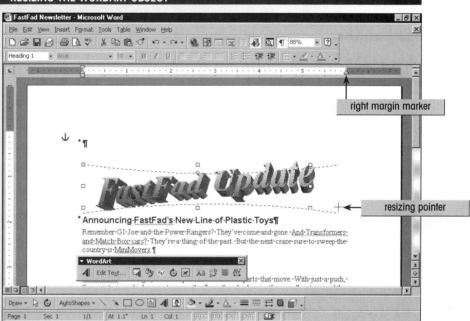

4. With the WordArt object still selected, click the **Free Rotate** button ⟳ on the WordArt toolbar. Round, green rotation handles surround the object.

5. Move the pointer anywhere on the document except over the WordArt text. The pointer changes to ⬚.

6. Position the pointer over the green circle on the lower-right corner of the object, and then drag the rotation handle clockwise about a half inch, or until the title text appears to be horizontal. See Figure 4-8.

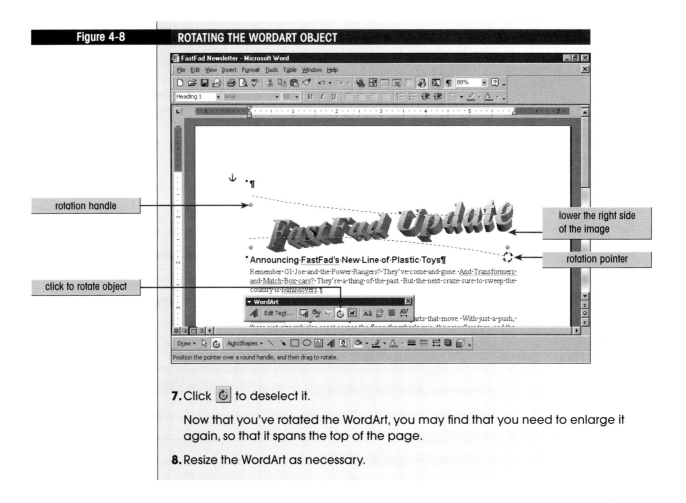

Figure 4-8 ROTATING THE WORDART OBJECT

7. Click 🔄 to deselect it.

Now that you've rotated the WordArt, you may find that you need to enlarge it again, so that it spans the top of the page.

8. Resize the WordArt as necessary.

Anchoring the WordArt

Now that you have sized and rotated the WordArt, you need to make sure it is properly positioned within the document as a whole—a process known as anchoring. The process draws its name from the **anchor** symbol in the left margin, which indicates the position of the WordArt relative to the text. To ensure that changes to the text (such as section breaks) do not affect the WordArt, you need to anchor the WordArt to a blank paragraph before the text. That is, you should make sure the anchor symbol is located to the left of, or just above, the paragraph symbol. Also, make sure that the paragraph mark is positioned below the WordArt image on the screen. Depending on exactly how you sized and rotated your WordArt, the anchor and paragraph symbols may or may not be in the proper position now. For instance, in Figure 4-8, the anchor is located just above the paragraph symbol, just as it should be. However, the paragraph symbol itself is located above the WordArt rather than below. It's up to you to decide if your WordArt is anchored properly.

To anchor the FastFad WordArt:

1. Drag the WordArt image up or down as necessary, until the anchor symbol and the paragraph symbol are positioned similarly to Figure 4-9.

| Figure 4-9 | PROPERLY ANCHORED WORDART |

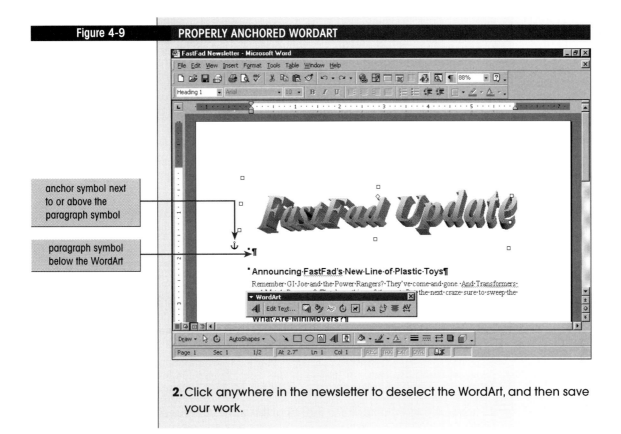

anchor symbol next to or above the paragraph symbol

paragraph symbol below the WordArt

2. Click anywhere in the newsletter to deselect the WordArt, and then save your work.

Your WordArt is now finished. The formatted WordArt title will draw the sales reps' attention to the newsletter as they review this document.

Formatting Text into Newspaper-Style Columns

Because newsletters are meant for quick reading, they usually are laid out in newspaper-style columns. In **newspaper-style columns**, a page is divided into two or more vertical blocks, or columns. Text flows down one column, continues at the top of the next column, flows down that column, and so forth. Newspaper-style columns are easier to read because the columns tend to be narrow and the type size is a bit smaller than the text in a letter. This enables the eye to see more text in one glance than when text is set in longer line lengths and in a larger font size.

If you want some of your text to be in columns and other text to be in full line lengths, you must insert section breaks into your document and apply the column format only to those sections you want in columns. You could select the text and use the Columns button on the Standard toolbar to automatically insert the needed section breaks and divide the text into columns. But because Gerrit wants you to divide the text below the title into two columns and add a vertical line between them, you'll use the Columns command on the Format menu. This lets you do both actions and insert a section break in the location you specify. Without the section break, the line between the columns would extend up through the title.

Formatting Text Into Newspaper-Style Columns

- Select the text you want to divide into columns, or don't select any text if you want the entire document divided into columns.
- Click the Columns button on the Standard toolbar, and highlight the number of columns you want to divide the text into.

  or

- Move the insertion point to the location where you want the columns to begin.
- Click Format on the menu bar, and then click Columns to open the Columns dialog box.
- Select the column style you want in the Presets section.
- Deselect the Line between check box if you do *not* want a vertical line between columns.
- If necessary, click the Equal column width check box to deselect it, and then set the width of each column in the Width and spacing section.
- Click the Apply to list arrow, and select This point forward if you want Word to insert a section break. Otherwise, select the Whole document option.
- If you want a vertical rule between the columns, click the Line between check box and click the OK button.

To apply newspaper-style columns to the body of the newsletter:

1. Position the insertion point to the left of the word "Announcing" just below the title.

2. Click **Format** on the menu bar, and then click **Columns**. The Columns dialog box opens.

3. In the Presets section, click the **Two** icon.

4. If necessary, click the **Line between** check box to select it. The text in the Preview box changes to a two-column format with a vertical rule between the columns.

   You want these changes to affect only the text after the title, so you'll need to insert a section break and apply the column formatting to the text after the insertion point.

5. Click the **Apply to** list arrow, and then click **This point forward** to have Word automatically insert a section break at the insertion point. See Figure 4-10.

Figure 4-10	COMPLETED COLUMNS DIALOG BOX

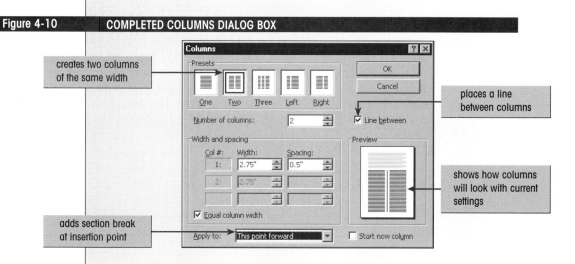

creates two columns of the same width

places a line between columns

shows how columns will look with current settings

adds section break at insertion point

6. Click the **OK** button to return to the document window. A section break appears, and the insertion point is now positioned in section 2. The text in section 2 is formatted in two columns.

TROUBLE? If the WordArt moves below the section break, drag it above the section break, and then click anywhere in the newsletter text to deselect the WordArt object.

Viewing the Whole Page

As you create a desktop-published document, you should periodically look at the whole page to get a sense of the overall layout. You can view the page in Print Preview as you've done before, or you can use the Zoom list arrow on the Standard toolbar to enlarge or reduce the percentage of the page you see onscreen.

To zoom out and view the whole page:

1. Click the **Zoom** list arrow on the Standard toolbar, and then click **Whole Page**. Word displays the entire page of the newsletter so you can see how the two-column format looks on the page. See Figure 4-11.

Figure 4-11	WHOLE PAGE VIEW SHOWING THE TWO COLUMNS

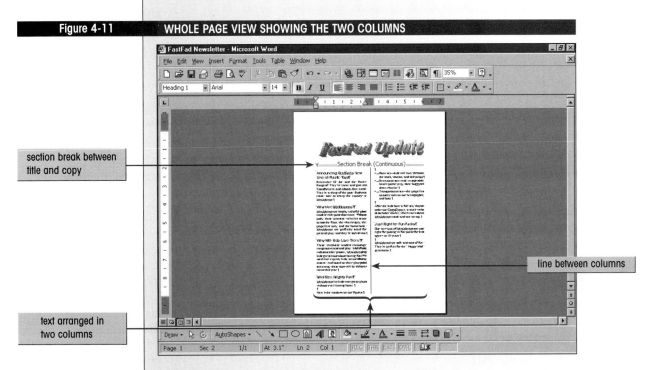

section break between title and copy

line between columns

text arranged in two columns

TROUBLE? Your columns may break at a slightly different line from those shown in the figure. This is not a problem; just continue with the tutorial.

The newsletter title is centered on the page, and the copy is in a two-column format. The text fills the left column but not the right column. You'll fix this later, after you add a graphic and format some of the text.

> **2.** Click the **Zoom** list arrow again, and then click **Page Width**. Now you can read the text again. Finally, you should save the document with a new name.
>
> **3.** Save the document as **FastFad Newsletter Copy 2** in the Tutorial folder for Tutorial 4.

You have set up an eye-catching title for the FastFad newsletter and formatted the text in newspaper-style columns to make it easier to read. Next, you will insert a graphic that illustrates the newsletter content. After you add clip art, you'll add more graphic interest by formatting some of the text. Then you'll finish the newsletter by making the columns equal in length and adding a border to the page.

Session 4.1 QUICK CHECK

1. Describe four elements commonly associated with desktop publishing.

2. In your own words, define the following terms:
   a. desktop publishing
   b. drawing object
   c. copy
   d. anchor

3. True or False: When using Word's desktop-publishing features, you should display your document in normal view.

4. True or False: Word treats WordArt the same way as any other document text.

5. How do you change the size of a WordArt object after you have inserted it into a Word document?

6. What is the purpose of the WordArt Shape button on the WordArt toolbar?

7. True or False: To format part of a document in newspaper-style columns, you need to insert a section break.

8. True or False: When you first format a document into newspaper-style columns, the columns will not necessarily be of equal length.

SESSION 4.2

In this session you will insert, resize, and crop clip art, and change the way the text wraps around the clip art. Then you'll create drop caps, insert typographic symbols, balance columns, place a border around the newsletter, and print the newsletter.

Inserting Clip Art

Graphics, which can include artwork, photographs, charts, tables, designs, or even designed text such as WordArt, add variety to documents and are especially appropriate for newsletters. Word allows you to draw pictures in your document, using the buttons on the Drawing toolbar. To produce professional-looking graphics, though, it's best to use one of two methods. In the first method, you begin by drawing a picture in a special graphics program or by scanning an existing image, such as a photograph. You can then save the graphic (often in a picture format known as a bitmapped graphic) and insert it into your document using the Picture command on the Insert menu. (You will have a chance to practice adding a bitmapped graphic to a document in Case Projects at the end of this tutorial.)

In the second method, you simply choose from a collection of pre-made, copyright-free images included along with Word. To add visual appeal to the FastFad newsletter, you will insert a piece of clip art now. Gerrit wants you to use a graphic that reflects the newsletter content.

REFERENCE   WINDOW   **RW**

<u>Working With Clip Art</u>
- Move the insertion point to the location in your document where you want the graphic image to appear.
- Click the Insert Clip Art button on the Drawing toolbar, or click Insert on the menu bar, point to Picture, and then click Clip Art to open the Insert ClipArt window.
- If necessary, click the Pictures tab.
- Click the category that best represents the type of art you need.
- Click the image you want to use.
- Click the Insert Clip icon.
- If you plan to use a particular clip art regularly, click the Add to Favorites or other category icon, verify that Favorites is selected in the list box, and then click OK. Click the Add to Favorites or other category icon again to hide the list box.
- To search for a particular image, type a description of the image you want in the Search for clips text box, and then press the Enter key.
- To re-display all the categories of clip art, click the All Categories button in the toolbar at the top of the Insert ClipArt window.
- To delete a graphic from a document, select it, and then press the Delete key.

To insert the clip-art image of an airplane into the newsletter:

1. If you took a break after the last session, make sure Word is running, the FastFad Newsletter is open, the document is in print layout view, and the nonprinting characters are displayed. Verify that the Drawing toolbar is displayed also.

2. Position the insertion point to the left of the word "MiniMovers" in the second paragraph of the newsletter just below the heading "What are MiniMovers?"

3. Click the **Insert Clip Art** button ⊠ on the Drawing toolbar. The Insert ClipArt window opens.

4. If necessary, click the **Pictures** tab.

5. Click the **All Categories** button to make sure all the clip art categories are displayed.

6. Scroll down and click the Transportation category. The Pictures tab now displays a variety of transportation-related images.

> **TROUBLE?** If you click the wrong category by mistake, click the All Categories button at the top of the Insert ClipArt window to redisplay all categories, and then click the Transportation category.

7. Scroll down, and click the airplane image. A menu of options opens, as shown in Figure 4-12.

Figure 4-12   **. PICTURES TAB OF THE INSERT CLIPART WINDOW**

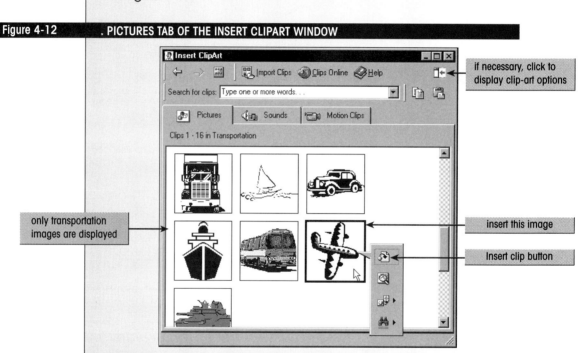

if necessary, click to display clip-art options

only transportation images are displayed

insert this image

Insert clip button

> **TROUBLE?** If your Insert ClipArt window is narrower than the one shown in Figure 4-12, click the Change to Full Window button at the top of the Insert ClipArt window, and then repeat Step 7.

8. Click the **Insert clip** button to insert the airplane in the newsletter at the insertion point.

9. Click the **Close** button to close the Insert ClipArt window.

10. Save the document. The airplane clip art fills the left column. The text below the heading moves down to make room for the image.

11. Click the airplane image to select it. Like the WordArt object you worked with earlier, the clip-art image is a graphic object with resize handles that you can use to change its size. The Picture toolbar appears whenever the clip-art object is selected. See Figure 4-13.

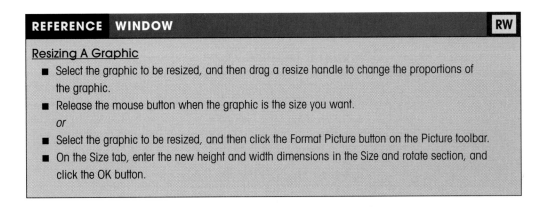

Figure 4-13 — **THE NEWSLETTER WITH THE CLIP ART OBJECT INSERTED**

Gerrit would like the image to be smaller so it doesn't distract attention from the text.

Resizing a Graphic

Often, you need to change the size of a graphic so that it fits into your document better. This is called **scaling** the image. You can resize a graphic by either dragging its resize handles or, for more precise control, by using the Format Picture dialog box.

REFERENCE WINDOW   RW

<u>Resizing A Graphic</u>
- Select the graphic to be resized, and then drag a resize handle to change the proportions of the graphic.
- Release the mouse button when the graphic is the size you want.
  or
- Select the graphic to be resized, and then click the Format Picture button on the Picture toolbar.
- On the Size tab, enter the new height and width dimensions in the Size and rotate section, and click the OK button.

For Gerrit's newsletter, the dragging technique will work fine.

To resize the clip-art graphic:

1. Make sure the clip-art graphic is selected, and scroll down so you can see the lower-right resize handle of the object.

2. Drag the lower-right resize handle up and to the left until the dotted outline forms a rectangle about 1.5 inches wide by 1.75 inches high. (Note that you don't have to hold down the Shift key, as you do with WordArt, to resize the picture proportionally.) See Figure 4-14.

| Figure 4-14 | RESIZING THE AIRPLANE GRAPHIC |

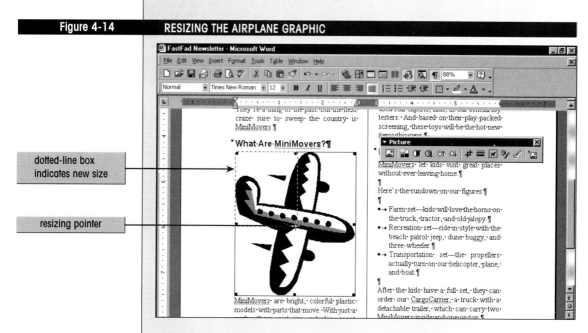

dotted-line box indicates new size

resizing pointer

3. Release the mouse button. The airplane image is now about half as wide as the first column.

Gerrit wonders if the airplane image would look better if you cut off the back end and showed only the front half.

Cropping a Graphic

You can **crop** the graphic—that is, cut off one or more of its edges—using either the Crop button on the Picture toolbar or the Format Picture dialog box. Once you crop a graphic, the part you cropped is hidden from view. It remains a part of the graphic image, though, so you can change your mind and restore a cropped graphic to its original form.

To crop the airplane graphic:

1. If necessary, click the clip art to select it. The resize handles appear.

2. Click the **Crop** button ⊞ on the Picture toolbar.

3. Position the pointer directly over the middle resize handle on the left side of the picture. The pointer changes to ⤧.

4. Press and hold down the mouse button, and drag the handle to the right so that only the wings and the nose of the plane are visible. See Figure 4-15.

Figure 4-15 CROPPING THE AIRPLANE GRAPHIC

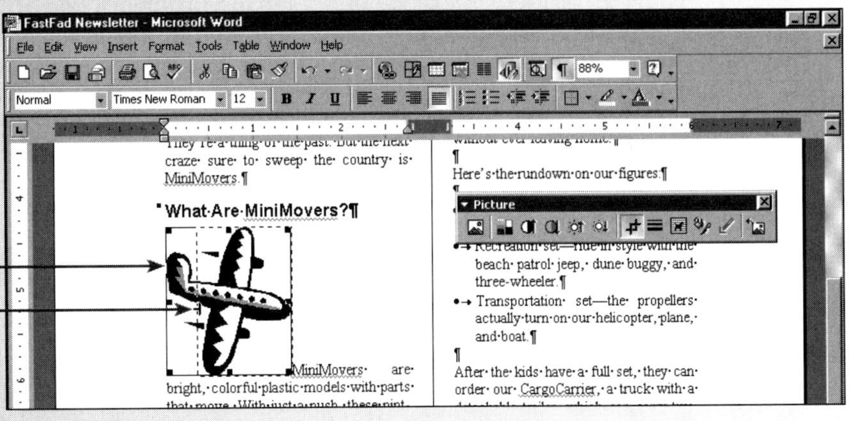

left half of image will be hidden from view

cropping pointer

5. Release the mouse button.

Gerrit decides he prefers to display the whole airplane, so he asks you to return to the original image.

6. Click the **Undo** button on the Standard toolbar. The cropping action is reversed, and the full image of the airplane reappears.

Now Gerrit wants you to make the text to wrap to the right of the graphic, making the airplane look as if it's flying into the text.

Wrapping Text Around a Graphic

For the airplane to look as though it flies into the newsletter text, you need to make the text wrap around the image. Earlier, you used text wrapping to position the WordArt title above the columns of text. Now you'll try a more advanced text-wrapping option to make the text follow the shape of the plane. You'll use the Format Picture dialog box to do this because it gives you more control over how the text flows around the picture.

To wrap text around the airplane graphic:

1. Verify that the airplane graphic is selected.

2. Click the **Format Picture** button on the Picture toolbar. The Format Picture dialog box opens.

3. Click the **Layout** tab. This tab contains a number of text-wrapping options, but to fine-tune the way text flows around the graphic, you need a more advanced set of options. You want the text to flow around the graphic, but only on the right side of the plane.

4. Click the **Advanced** button. The Advanced Layout dialog box opens.

5. Click the **Text Wrapping** tab, if necessary.

6. In the Wrapping style section, click the **Tight** icon, the second icon from the left.

7. In the Wrap text section, click the **Right only** option button. This option ensures that all text will flow to the right of the graphic. If you had used the options in the Layout tab (which you saw in Step 4), some of the text would have flowed into the white space to the left of the airplane, making the text difficult to read.

8. In the Distance from text section, click the **Right** up arrow once to display 0.2". Don't worry about the Left setting because the text will wrap only around the right side.

9. Click the **OK** button. You return to the Format Picture dialog box.

10. Click the **OK** button. The Format Picture dialog box closes.

11. Scroll down, if necessary, to view the picture. The text wraps to the right of the airplane, following its shape.

12. Click anywhere in the text to deselect the graphic, and then save the newsletter. Your screen should look similar to Figure 4-16.

| Figure 4-16 | TEXT WRAPPED AROUND GRAPHIC |

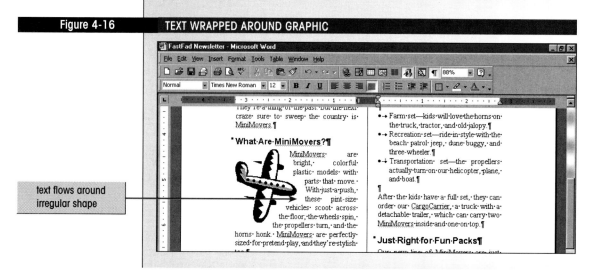

text flows around irregular shape

The image of the airplane draws the reader's attention to the beginning of the newsletter, but the rest of the text looks plain. Gerrit suggests adding a drop cap at the beginning of each section.

Inserting Drop Caps

A **drop cap** is a large, uppercase (capital) letter that highlights the beginning of the text of a newsletter, chapter, or some other document section. The drop cap usually extends from the top of the first line of the paragraph down two or three succeeding lines of the paragraph. The text of the paragraph wraps around the drop cap. Word allows you to create a drop cap for the first letter of the first word of a paragraph.

You will create a drop cap for the first paragraph following each heading in the newsletter (except for the first heading, where the clip-art image is located). The drop cap will extend two lines into the paragraph.

To insert drop caps in the newsletter:

1. Click in the paragraph following the first heading that starts with the word "Remember."

2. Click **Format** on the menu bar, and then click **Drop Cap**. The Drop Cap dialog box opens.

3. In the Position section, click the **Dropped** icon.

4. Click the **Lines to** drop down arrow once to display 2. You don't need to change the default distance from the text. See Figure 4-17.

Figure 4-17   DROP CAP DIALOG BOX

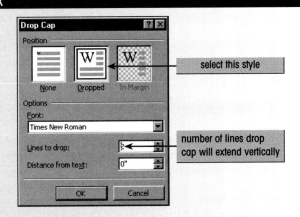

select this style

number of lines drop cap will extend vertically

5. Click the **OK** button to close the dialog box, then click anywhere in the newsletter to deselect the new drop cap. Word formats the first character of the paragraph as a drop cap.

6. Click anywhere in the newsletter text to deselect the drop cap. See Figure 4-18.

Figure 4-18	DROP CAP BEGINS THE PARAGRAPH

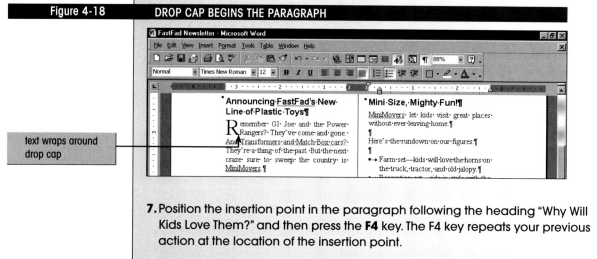

text wraps around drop cap

7. Position the insertion point in the paragraph following the heading "Why Will Kids Love Them?" and then press the **F4** key. The F4 key repeats your previous action at the location of the insertion point.

TROUBLE? If something else changes when you press the F4 key, you pressed another key or performed another action after Step 6. Click the Undo button on the Standard toolbar, position the insertion point in the next paragraph to which you want to add a drop cap, and then repeat Steps 2 though 6 for the paragraph specified in Step 7.

8. Repeat Step 7 for the text under the remaining two headings. Don't use a drop cap in the paragraph with the airplane image because it would make the paragraph difficult to read. If necessary, use the horizontal scroll bar to bring the second column into view.

The newsletter looks more lively with the drop caps. Next, you turn your attention to the issue of inserting a registered trademark symbol beside the trademark names.

Inserting Symbols and Special Characters

Gerrit used standard word-processing characters rather than **typographic characters** (special symbols and punctuation marks) when he typed the newsletter copy. For example, he typed two dashes in place of an em dash. Word's AutoCorrect feature converts some of these standard characters (such as the dashes) into more polished-looking typographic symbols as you type. Figure 4-19 lists some of the characters that AutoCorrect automatically converts to symbols. In some cases, you need to press the spacebar before Word will convert the characters to the appropriate symbol.

Figure 4-19	COMMON TYPOGRAPHICAL SYMBOLS		
TO INSERT THIS SYMBOL OR CHARACTER	**TYPE**	**WORD CONVERTS IT TO**	
em dash	word--word	word—word	
smiley	:)	☺	
copyright symbol	(c)	©	
registered trademark symbol	(r)	®	
trademark symbol	(tm)	™	
ordinal numbers	1st, 2nd, 3rd, etc.	1ST, 2ND, 3RD, etc.	
fractions	1/2, 1/4	½, ¼	
arrows	--> or <--	→ or ←	

To insert typographic characters into a document after you've finished typing it, you also can use the Symbol command on the Insert menu.

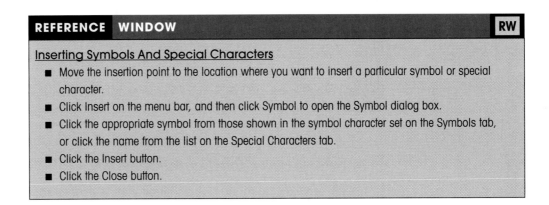

REFERENCE WINDOW   **RW**

<u>Inserting Symbols And Special Characters</u>
- Move the insertion point to the location where you want to insert a particular symbol or special character.
- Click Insert on the menu bar, and then click Symbol to open the Symbol dialog box.
- Click the appropriate symbol from those shown in the symbol character set on the Symbols tab, or click the name from the list on the Special Characters tab.
- Click the Insert button.
- Click the Close button.

To make the newsletter look professionally formatted, you'll insert two special characters now—a registered trademark symbol and a trademark symbol—at the appropriate places.

FastFad protects the names of its products by registering the names as trademarks. You'll indicate that in the newsletter by inserting the registered trademark symbol (®) at the first occurrence of the trademark name "MiniMovers" and a trademark symbol (™) for the first occurrence of "CargoCarrier."

To insert the registered trademark symbol:

1. Position the insertion point at the end of the word "MiniMovers" in the first paragraph, just before the period.

2. Click **Insert** on the menu bar, and then click **Symbol** to open the Symbol dialog box.

3. If necessary, click the **Special Characters** tab. See Figure 4-20.

Figure 4-20 | **SPECIAL CHARACTERS TAB IN SYMBOL DIALOG BOX**

click to display this tab →

insert this symbol →

4. Click **Registered** to select it, and then click the **Insert** button. The dialog box stays open so you can insert additional symbols and characters in this location.

5. Click the **Close** button to close the Symbol dialog box. Word has inserted ® immediately after the word "MiniMovers."

If you have to insert symbols repeatedly, or if you want to insert them quickly as you type, it's often easier to use the Word AutoCorrect feature to insert them. You'll use AutoCorrect now to insert the trademark symbol (™) after the first occurrence of CargoCarrier. First, you'll look in the AutoCorrect settings to make sure the correct entry is there.

To enter a symbol using AutoCorrect:

1. Click **Tools** on the menu bar, and then click **AutoCorrect**. The AutoCorrect tab of the AutoCorrect dialog box opens. In the Replace column on the left side of the dialog box, you see (tm), which means that any occurrence of (tm) in the document will change to the trademark symbol. Now that you know the symbol is there, you'll try entering it in the document.

2. Click the **Cancel** button.

3. Position the insertion point just after the word "CargoCarrier" in the second column, in the paragraph above the heading "Just Right for Fun Packs."

4. Type **(tm)**. Word converts your typed characters into the trademark symbol.

The trademark symbols ensure that everyone who reads the newsletter is aware that these names are protected. Next, you decide to adjust the columns of text so they are approximately the same lengths.

Balancing the Columns

You could shift text from one column to another by adding blank paragraphs to move the text into the next column or by deleting blank paragraphs to shorten the text so it will fit into one column. The problem with this approach is that any edits you make could throw off the balance. Instead, Word can automatically balance the columns, or make them of equal length.

To balance the columns:

1. Position the insertion point at the end of the text in the right column, just after the period following the word "generation." Next, you need to change the zoom to Whole Page so you can see the full effect of the change.

2. Click the **Zoom** list arrow on the Standard toolbar, and then click **Whole Page**.

3. Click **Insert** on the menu bar, and then click **Break**. The Break dialog box opens.

4. Below "section break types," click the **Continuous** option button.

5. Click the **OK** button. Word inserts a continuous section break at the end of the text, which, along with the first section break you inserted earlier, defines the area in which it should balance the columns. As shown in Figure 4-21, Word balances the text between the two section breaks.

Figure 4-21	NEWSLETTER WITH BALANCED COLUMNS

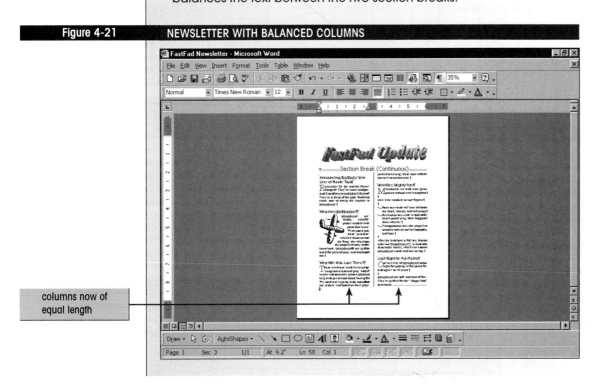

columns now of equal length

Drawing a Border Around the Page

Gerrit wants to give the newsletter a little more pizzazz. He suggests adding a border around the newsletter.

To draw a border around the newsletter:

1. Make sure the document is in print layout view and that the zoom setting is set to Whole Page so that you can see the entire newsletter.

2. Click **Format** on the menu bar, and then click **Borders and Shading**. The Borders and Shading dialog box opens.

3. Click the **Page Border** tab. You can use the Setting options, on the left side, to specify the type of border you want. In this case, you want a simple box.

4. In the Setting section, click the **Box** option. Now that you have selected the type of border you want, you can choose the style of line that will be used to create the border.

5. In the Style list box, scroll down and select the ninth style down from the top (the thick line with the thin line underneath), and then verify that the Apply to list option is set to Whole document. See Figure 4-22.

| Figure 4-22 | BORDERS AND SHADING DIALOG BOX |

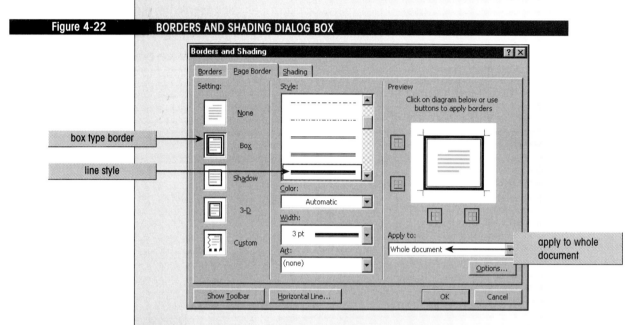

6. Click **OK**. The newsletter is now surrounded by an attractive border, as shown in Figure 4-23.

| Figure 4-23 | FINISHED NEWSLETTER |

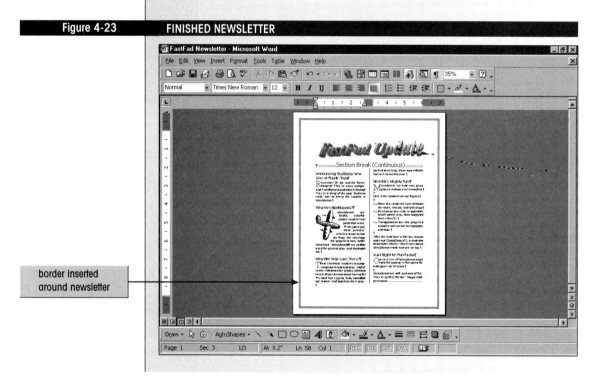

7. Save the completed newsletter as **FastFind Newsletter Final Copy** in the Tutorial folder for Tutorial 4.

8. Create a footer that centers "Prepared by *your name*" at the bottom of the document. Be sure to replace *your name* with your first and last name. Format the footer in a small font to make it as unobtrusive as possible.

9. Preview the newsletter and then print it. Unless you have a color printer, the orange and yellow letters of the title and the airplane will print in black and white.

10. If necessary, click the **Close** button on the Print Preview toolbar to return to print layout view, then close the newsletter and exit Word.

You give the printed newsletter to Gerrit, along with a copy on disk. He thinks it looks great and thanks you for your help. He'll print it later on a high-quality color printer (to get the best resolution for printing multiple copies) and distribute the newsletter to FastFad's sales staff.

Session 4.2 QUICK CHECK

1. Define the following in your own words:

    a. drop cap
    b. scaling
    c. clip art
    d. balance

2. Explain how to insert a clip-art graphic in Word.

3. Describe a situation in which you would want to scale a graphic. Describe a situation in which you would want to crop a graphic.

4. True or False: When inserting a drop cap, you can specify the number of lines you want the drop cap to extend into the document vertically.

5. Describe two different methods for inserting the registered trademark symbol in a document.

6. Besides the Symbol command on the Insert menu, what is another way of entering typographic symbols?

7. Describe the process for drawing a border around the page.

REVIEW ASSIGNMENTS

Gerrit's FastFad newsletter was a success; the sales representatives all seemed to have good product knowledge, and the sales for MiniMovers were brisk. Now the sales reps want a product information sheet (similar to the newsletter) about another product, FastFad Action Pros, that they can print and send directly to their clients. You'll create that newsletter now.

1. If necessary, start Word and make sure your Data Disk is in the appropriate disk drive. Check your screen to make sure your settings match those in the tutorial and that the nonprinting characters and Drawing toolbar are displayed.

2. Open the file **FigSpecs** from the Review folder for Tutorial 4 on your Data Disk, and then save it as **Action Pros**.

3. In the second-to-last line of the document, replace "our toll free-number" with your name.

4. Click the Insert WordArt button on the Drawing toolbar.

5. Choose the WordArt style in the fourth row down, second column from the left.

6. Type "FastFad Pros" in the Edit WordArt Text dialog box, and then click OK.

7. Drag the WordArt above the first heading so that the anchor symbol is positioned to the left of the first paragraph symbol and so that the paragraph symbol is positioned below the WordArt on the screen.

8. Use the WordArt Shape button on the WordArt toolbar to apply the Inflate shape (fourth row down, leftmost column).

9. Click the Edit Text button on the WordArt toolbar and change the font to 32-point Times New Roman bold.

10. Use the Text Wrapping button on the WordArt toolbar to apply the Top and Bottom wrapping style.

11. Drag the lower-right and then the lower-left resize handles to enlarge the image to span the entire width between the left and right margins. Be sure to hold down the Shift key while you drag. Size the WordArt to make it approximately two-inches tall.

12. Save the document.

13. Position the insertion point to the left of the first word in the first heading, and then format the text into two columns using the Columns dialog box. Insert a section break so that the columns appear from this point forward. Do not insert a line between columns.

14. View the whole newsletter in print layout view, using the Whole Page zoom setting.

15. Return to Page Width zoom, and then position the insertion point at the beginning of the first paragraph, right before the phrase "FastFad Action Pros are the latest…".

16. Use the Insert Clip Art button on the Drawing toolbar to insert the baseball player clip-art image from the Sports & Leisure category.

17. Select and resize the sports image so it fits in the left half of the first column.

18. Click the Crop button on the Picture toolbar, and then try cropping the image horizontally and vertically by dragging the appropriate selection handles.

19. Use the Undo button to uncrop the image.

20. Select the picture, click the Format Picture button on the Picture toolbar, click the Layout tab, and then click the Advanced button. Set the Wrapping style to Tight, and wrap the text around the right side of the image.

21. Format a drop cap for the first paragraph following the "Five Sets of Figures" heading, using the default settings for the Dropped position.

22. Insert the trademark symbol after the first occurrence of "FastFad Action Pros."

Explore 23. As you might have noticed, Word automatically justifies text in newspaper columns, but you can easily change that alignment. Select both columns of text by clicking before the first word of text ("Product"), pressing and holding down the Shift key, and then clicking after the last word of text in the second column ("business"). Use the Align Left button on the Formatting toolbar to change the columns' text alignment to left alignment.

24. Make the columns of equal length by balancing the columns. Position the insertion point at the end of the document, click Insert on the menu bar, and then click Break. Below Section break types, click the Continuous option button, and then click the OK button.

Explore   25. A pull quote is a phrase or quotation taken from the text that summarizes a key point. To insert a pull quote, click the Text Box button on the Drawing toolbar, and then drag the pointer below the two columns to draw a text box that spans the page width and fills the space between the columns and the bottom margin. Use the Enter key to center the insertion point vertically in the text box. Type "FastFad: Playing is our business." Now format the text in the text box as 18-point Times New Roman italic, bold, and then use the Center button to center the text horizontally in the box.

Explore   26. You can use the Replace command to replace standard word-processing characters with typographic characters. To replace every occurrence of -- (two dashes) with — (an em dash), position the insertion point at the beginning of the first paragraph of text. Click Edit on the menu bar, and then click Replace. In the Find what text box, type "--" (two hyphens), and then press the Tab key to move the insertion point to the Replace with text box. Click the More button to display additional options and then click the Special button at the bottom of the dialog box. Click Em Dash in the list to display the special code Word has for em dashes in the Replace with text box. Click the Replace All button. When the operation is complete, click the OK button, and then click the Close button.

27. Add a border to the page using the Page Border command and the line style of your choice.

28. Look at the newsletter in print layout view, using the Whole Page zoom setting.

29. Preview, save, and print the document.

CASE PROBLEMS

Case 1. **City of Madison, Wisconsin**   Claudia Mora is the manager of information systems for the city of Madison. She and her staff, along with the city manager, have just decided to convert all city computers from the Windows 3.1 operating system to Windows 98 and to standardize applications software on Microsoft Office 2000. Claudia writes a monthly newsletter on computer operations and training, so this month she decides to devote the newsletter to the conversion to Windows 98 and Microsoft Office 2000.

1. If necessary, start Word, make sure your Data Disk is in the appropriate drive, and check your screen to make sure your settings match those in the tutorial.

2. Open the file **CityComp** from the Cases folder for Tutorial 4 on your Data Disk, and then save the file as **Computer**.

Explore   3. If the text you want to format as WordArt has already been typed, you can cut it from the document and paste it into the WordArt dialog box. You can try this technique now. Cut the text of the newsletter title, "Computer News." Click the Insert WordArt button on the Drawing toolbar, and then choose the WordArt style in the third row down, second column from the left. Paste the text (using the Ctrl+V shortcut keys) into the Edit WordArt Text dialog box, and then click OK.

4. Drag the WordArt to the top of the newsletter, so that the anchor symbol is positioned to the left of the first paragraph symbol, and set the wrapping style to Top and Bottom.

5. In the Edit WordArt Text dialog box, set the font to 32-point Arial bold, then use the WordArt Shape button on the Drawing toolbar to apply the Arch Up (Curve) shape.

Explore   6. Experiment with changing the shape of the WordArt object by dragging the yellow adjustment handle.

7. Resize the WordArt object so that it spans the width of the page from left margin to right margin and so that its maximum height is about 1 inch. (*Hint:* Use the resize handles while watching the horizontal and vertical rulers in print layout view to adjust the object to the appropriate size.)

8. Center and italicize the subtitle of the newsletter, "Newsletter from the Madison Information Management Office."

9. Replace "INSERT YOUR NAME HERE" with your name, then center and italicize it.

10. Insert a continuous section break before the subtitle. (*Hint:* The section break may appear above the WordArt title, depending on where the anchor is positioned, but this is not a problem.)

Explore   11. To emphasize the subtitle paragraph with the city name, insert a border around all four sides and shade the paragraph using the Borders and Shading command. (*Hint:* In the Borders and Shading dialog box, click the Shading tab, select a light, see-through color from the Fill grid, such as Gray-15%, and then click OK.)

12. Move the insertion point to the beginning of the heading "The Big Switch." Then format the body of the newsletter into two newspaper-style columns; set the format of the columns so that no vertical rule appears between the columns. Use the This point forward option in the Apply to list box to make the columns a separate section.

13. Position the insertion point at the beginning of the first paragraph under the heading "Training on MS Office 2000," and insert the clip-art image from the Business category that shows a person using a laptop computer in front of a group.

Explore   14. Resize the picture so that it is 35 percent of its original size. Instead of dragging the resize handles as you did in the tutorial, use the Size tab in the Format Picture dialog box to scale the image. Adjust the Height and Width settings to 35 percent in the Scale section, and make sure the Lock aspect ratio check box is selected.

Explore   15. Click the Text Wrapping button on the Picture toolbar and select the Tight option.

16. Replace any double hyphens with typographic em dashes.

17. Make sure the newsletter fits on one page; if necessary, decrease the height of the WordArt title until the newsletter fits on one page.

18. Insert a border around the newsletter.

19. If necessary, balance the columns.

20. Save and print the newsletter, and then close it.

Case 2. *Morning Star Movers* Martin Lott is the executive secretary to Whitney Kremer, director of personnel for Morning Star Movers (MSM), a national moving company with headquarters in Minneapolis, Minnesota. Whitney assigned you the task of preparing the monthly newsletter News and Views, which provides news about MSM employees. You decide to update the layout and to use the desktop-publishing capabilities of Word to design the newsletter. You will use text assembled by other MSM employees for the body of the newsletter.

1. If necessary, start Word, make sure your Data Disk is in the appropriate drive, and check your screen to make sure your settings match those in the tutorial.

2. Open the file **MSM_NEWS** from the Cases folder for Tutorial 4 on your Data Disk, and then save it as **MSM Newsletter**.

3. Use the Find and Replace command to replace all instances of the name "Katrina" with your first name. Then replace all instances of "Pollei" with your last name.

4. Create a "News and Views" WordArt title for the newsletter, and set the font to 24-point Arial bold. Use the WordArt style in the third row, fourth column from the left, and set the shape of the text to Wave 2 (third row, sixth column from the left).

5. Drag the WordArt title to the top of the newsletter so that the anchor symbol is positioned to the left of the first paragraph symbol, and set the wrapping style to Top and Bottom.

6. Resize the WordArt proportionally so that the title spans the width of the page from left margin to right margin and so that the height of the title is about 1 inch. (*Hint:* Use the resize handles while watching the horizontal and vertical rulers in print layout view to adjust the object to the appropriate size.)

7. Format the body of the newsletter into two newspaper-style columns, and place a vertical rule between the columns.

Explore   8. You can change the structure of a newsletter by reformatting it with additional columns. Change the number of columns from two to three using the same technique you used in the previous step (that is, the Columns command on the Format menu). Make sure that the Equal column width check box is selected.

Explore   9. You can insert your own bitmapped graphics, stored on a disk, just as easily as you can insert clip art. Position the insertion point at the beginning of the paragraph below the heading "MSM Chess Team Takes Third." Click Insert on the menu bar, point to Picture, and then click From File. Look in the Cases folder for Tutorial 4 on your Data Disk, select the file named **Knight**, and then click the Insert button.

Explore   10. You can easily delete a graphic by selecting it, and then pressing the Delete key. To practice this technique, click the Knight graphic to select it, and then press the Delete key. To reinsert the graphic, click the Undo button.

Explore   11. Scale the height and the width of the picture to 60 percent of its original size. (*Hint:* To scale the size, use the Format Picture button on the Picture toolbar, and then set the Scale values on the Size tab, making sure the Lock aspect ratio check box is selected.)

Explore   12. Use the Picture tab in the Format Picture dialog box, and change the values in the Crop from text boxes. Crop 0.3, 0.4, 0.2, and 0.4 inches from the left, right, top, and bottom of the picture, respectively.

13. Wrap the text around the clip art.

14. Format drop caps in the first paragraph after each heading except the "MSM Chess Team Takes Third" heading. Use the default settings for number of lines, but change the font of the drop cap to Arial.

15. View the entire page. If necessary, decrease the height of the WordArt title or change the page margins until the entire newsletter fits onto one page and until each column starts with a heading.

16. Add a border around the entire page of the newsletter using the Page Border command.

17. Save the newsletter, and then preview and print it. Close the document.

Case 3. Lake Mendota Wellness Clinic The Lake Mendota Wellness Clinic, located in Vicksburg, Mississippi, is a private company that contracts with small and large businesses to promote health and fitness among their employees. Mary Anne Logan, an exercise physiologist, is director of health and fitness at the clinic. As part of her job, she writes a newsletter for the employees of the companies with which the clinic contracts. She's asked you to transform her document into a polished, desktop-published newsletter.

1. If necessary, start Word, make sure your Data Disk is in the appropriate drive, and check your screen to make sure your settings match those in the tutorials.

2. Open the file **Wellness** from the Cases folder for Tutorial 4 on your Data Disk, and then save it as **Wellness Newsletter**.

3. In the third line, replace "YOUR NAME HERE" with your first and last names.

4. At the beginning of the newsletter, create a WordArt title "Feeling Good." Choose any WordArt style that you feel would be appropriate to the newsletter content, and set the font to 24-point, italic Times New Roman.

5. Set the shape of the text to any option that looks appropriate to the subject matter.

6. Move the title to the top of the document, so the anchor symbol is positioned to the left of the first paragraph symbol.

Explore 7. Add a shadow to the WordArt title (or adjust the existing one) by clicking the Shadow button on the Drawing toolbar and selecting a Shadow option. Then use the Shadow Settings option on the Shadow button to open the Shadow Settings toolbar. Click the Shadow Color button on the Shadow Settings toolbar, select a good color for the shadow, then close the Shadow Settings toolbar. For the purpose of this exercise, choose a shadow style that is behind the text, not in front of it.

Explore 8. Rotate the WordArt 90 degrees. (*Hint:* In the Format WordArt dialog box, click the Size tab and set the Rotation option to 90 degrees.)

Explore 9. Resize the WordArt graphic box so that the WordArt object spans the height of the page from the top margin to the bottom margin and the width of the object is about 1 inch. (*Hint:* Use the resize handles while watching the horizontal and vertical rulers in print layout view to adjust the object to the appropriate size.)

10. Drag the WordArt object to the right edge of the page.

11. Use the Advanced wrapping options to change the Wrapping style to Square and Left only.

12. At the top of the page, italicize the subtitles, the line that contains the issue volume and number of the newsletter, and the line that contains your name.

13. Format the body of the newsletter as a separate section, in two newspaper-style columns with a vertical rule between the columns. (*Hint:* The columns' widths will be uneven because the WordArt title takes up part of the second column space.)

14. To the right of each of the words "NordicTrack" and "HealthRider," insert a registered trademark symbol (®), and then change the font size of the symbol to 8 points. (*Hint:* Highlight the symbol and change the font size.)

15. Balance the columns.

16. Save the newsletter, and then preview and print it. Close the document.

Case 4. New Home Newsletter You've just moved to a new part of the country and decide to send out a newsletter to friends and family describing your new home. In the one-page newsletter, you'll include articles about you and your family or friends, your new job, your new abode, and future plans. You'll desktop publish the copy into a professional-looking newsletter.

1. If necessary, start Word, make sure your Data Disk is in the appropriate drive, and check your screen to make sure your settings match those in the tutorials.

2. Write two articles to include in the newsletter; save each article in a separate file.

3. Plan the general layout of your newsletter.

4. Create a title ("New Home News") for your newsletter with WordArt.

5. Save the document as **New Home** in the Cases folder for Tutorial 4.

6. Insert the current date and your name as editor below the title.

Explore 7. Insert the articles you wrote into your newsletter. Position the insertion point where you want the first article to appear, click Insert on the menu bar, click File, select the article you want to insert, and then click the Insert button. Repeat to insert the second article.

8. Format your newsletter with multiple columns.

9. Insert at least one clip-art picture into your newsletter, and wrap text around it.

10. Format at least two drop caps in the newsletter.

Explore 11. Create a border around the page and then add shading to the entire document using the Shading and Borders command on the Format menu. (*Hint:* Click CTRL+A to select the entire document, open the Borders and Shading dialog box, select a page border, click the Shading tab, select a light, see-through color from the Fill grid, such as Gray-15%, and then click OK.)

12. Save and print the newsletter, and then close the document.

INTERNET ASSIGNMENTS

The purpose of the Internet Assignments is to challenge you to find information on the Internet that you can use to create effective documents. The actual assignments are updated and maintained on the Course Technology Web site. Log on to the Internet and use your Web browser to go to the Student Online Companion to accompany this text at **www.course.com/NewPerspectives/office2000**. Click the Word link, and then click the link for Tutorial 4.

Quick │ Check Answers

Session 4.1

1. (list 4) The printing is high-quality; the document uses multiple fonts; the document incorporates graphics; the document uses typographic characters; the document uses columns and other special formatting features.

2. (a) Using a desktop computer system to producing commercial-quality printed material. With desktop publishing you can enter and edit text, create graphics, lay out pages, and print documents. (b) An image whose appearance you can change using the Drawing toolbar or WordArt toolbar (c) The unformatted text of a newsletter (d) A symbol that appears in the left margin, which shows a WordArt object's position in relation to the text

3. False

4. False

5. To resize a WordArt object, select the object and drag its resize handles. To resize the WordArt object proportionally, press and hold the Shift key as you drag a resize handle.

6. The WordArt Shape button allows you to change the basic shape of a WordArt object.

7. True

8. True

Session 4.2

1. (a) a large, uppercase letter that highlights the beginning of the text of a newsletter, chapter, or some other document section; (b) resizing an image to better fit a document; (c) existing, copyright-free artwork that you can insert into your document; (d) to make columns of equal length

2. Position the insertion point at the location where you want to insert the image, click the Insert Clip Art button on the Drawing toolbar, click the Pictures tab in the Insert ClipArt window, click the category that best represents the type of art you need, click the image you want to use, click the Insert clip button.

3. You might scale a graphic to better fit the width of a column of text. You might crop a graphic to emphasize or draw attention to a particular part of the image or to eliminate unnecessary borders.

4. True

5. Click where you want to insert the symbol in the document, click Insert on the menu bar, click Symbol, click the Special Characters tab in the Symbol dialog box, click Registered Trademark in the list, click the Insert button, and then click the Close button. Type (tm).

6. Using the AutoCorrect feature, which lets you type certain characters and then changes those characters into the corresponding symbol

7. Click Format on the menu bar, click Borders and Shading, click the Page Border tab in the Borders and Shading dialog box, select the border type you want in the Setting section, choose a line style from the Style list box, make sure Whole document appears in the Apply to list box, and then click OK.

INDEX

TASK	PAGE #	RECOMMENDED METHOD
Action, redo	WD 2.11	Click ↻
Action, undo	WD 2.11	Click ↺
Border, draw around page	WD 4.25	Click Format, click Borders and Shading, click Page Border tab, click Box, apply to Whole Document
Bullets, add to paragraphs	WD 2.25	Select paragraphs, click ☰
Clip art, insert	WD 4.15	Click ▦ on Drawing toolbar, click Pictures tab, click the category you want, click the image you want, click ⬇
Clipboard, erase contents of	WD 2.15	Click ✕
Column break, insert	WD 4.25	Click Insert, click Break, click Column Break, click OK
Columns, balance	WD 4.24	Insert column break or click the end of the column, click Insert, click Break, click Continuous, click OK
Columns, format text in	WD 4.11	Select the text, click Format, click Columns, select the column style you want in the Presets section, click OK
Document, close	WD 1.30	If more than one document is open, click ✕ on title bar; if only one document is open, click ✕ on menu bar
Document, create new	WD 1.13	Click ▯
Document, open	WD 2.02	Click ☍, select drive and folder, click the filename, click OK
Document, preview	WD 1.26	Click ▤
Document, print	WD 1.27	Click ▤, or click File, click Print, specify pages or number of copies, click OK
Document, save	WD 1.17	Click ▦
Document, save with new name	WD 2.05	Click File, click Save As, select drive and folder, enter new filename, click Save
Drop cap, insert	WD 4.20	Position insertion point in paragraph, click Format, click Drop Cap, select desired features, click OK
Envelope, print	WD 1.29	Click Tools, click Envelopes and Labels, click Envelopes tab, type delivery and return addresses, click Print
File Properties, add	WD 1.19	Click File, click Properties, click Summary tab, add desired information, click OK
Font size, change	WD 2.27	Select text, click Font Size list arrow, click new font size
Font style, change	WD 2.29	Select text, click **B**, *I*, or <u>U</u>
Font, change	WD 2.27	Select text, click Font list arrow, click new font
Footer, insert	WD 3.10	Click View, click Header and Footer, click ▤, type footer text, click Close
Format Painter, use	WD 2.24	Select text with desired format, double-click ✎, click paragraphs you want to format, click ✎

TASK	PAGE #	RECOMMENDED METHOD
Graphic, crop	WD 4.18	Click graphic, click ⊞ on Picture toolbar, drag resize handle
Graphic, resize	WD 4.17	Click graphic, drag resize handle
Graphic, wrap text around	WD 4.19	Select graphic, then click ⊞ on Picture toolbar and select option or click ⊞ on Picture toolbar, click Layout tab, click Advanced, click Text Wrapping tab, select Wrapping style option, set Distance from text, click OK twice
Header, insert	WD 3.10	Click View, click Header and Footer, type header text, click Close
Help, get	WD 1.28	Click ⊞ and type a question, click Search, click topic
Line spacing, change	WD 2.20	Select the text you want to change, then press CTRL+1 for single spacing, CTRL+5 for 1.5 line spacing, or CTRL+2 for double spacing
Margins, change	WD 2.18	Click File, click Page Setup, click Margins tab, enter margin values, click OK
Nonprinting characters,	WD 1.10	Click ¶
Normal view, change to	WD 1.07	Click ≡
Numbering, add to paragraphs	WD 2.25	Select paragraphs, click ⊞
Office Assistant, close	WD 1.28	Click Help, click Hide Office Assistant
Office Assistant, open	WD 1.28	Click ⊞
Page, move to top of next	WD 3.12	Click ⊞
Page, move to top of previous	WD 3.12	Click ⊞
Page, view whole	WD 4.13	Click Zoom list arrow, click Whole Page
Page break, insert	WD 3.15	Position insertion point at break location, press Ctrl+Enter
Page number, insert	WD 3.12	Switch to header or footer, click ⊞ on Header and Footer toolbar
Paragraph, change indent	WD 2.23	Select paragraph, drag left or first-line indent marker on ruler; click ⊞ or ⊞
Print layout view, change to	WD 3.12	Click ⊞
Ruler, display	WD 1.09	Click View, click Ruler
Section break, create	WD 3.06	Position insertion point at break location, click Insert, click Break, click Section break types option button, click OK
Section, vertically align	WD 3.07	Move insertion point into section, click File, click Page Setup, click Layout tab, click Apply to list arrow, click This section, click Vertical alignment list arrow, click desired option, click OK
Shading, insert	WD 4.30	Click Format, click Borders and Shading, click Shading tab, select Fill and Pattern options, click OK
Spelling, correct	WD 1.23	Right-click misspelled word (as indicated by red wavy underline), click correctly spelled word

TASK	PAGE #	RECOMMENDED METHOD
Spelling and grammar, correct	WD 2.05	Click at the beginning of the document, click [icon], review any errors, accept suggestions or ignore errors as desired; to type corrections directly in the document, click outside the Spelling and Grammar dialog box, make the desired correction, and then click Resume in the Spelling and Grammar dialog box
Symbol, insert	WD 4.22	Click Insert, click Symbol, click desired symbol, click Insert, click Close
Tab stop, set	WD 3.04	Click tab alignment selector to select desired tab alignment style, click horizontal ruler where you want to insert tab stop
Table cells, merge	WD 3.23	Select cells you want to merge, click [icon] on Tables and Borders toolbar
Table cells, split	WD 3.23	Select cells you want to split, click [icon] on Tables and Borders toolbar, specify the number of cells or rows into which you want to divide the cell, click OK
Table column width, change	WD 3.24	Position pointer over column's right border, press and hold down ALT and mouse button, drag to adjust column width to desired measurement as indicated in horizontal ruler
Table gridlines, display	WD 3.29	Select table, click Table, click Show Gridlines
Table, sum cells of	WD 3.23	Click cell where you want sum, click [icon] on Tables and Borders toolbar
Table row, align text horizontally in	WD 3.27	Select a cell or range, click [icon], [icon], [icon], or [icon]
Table row, align text vertically in	WD 3.27	Select row, click alignment list arrow on Tables and Borders toolbar, click desired alignment
Table row height, change	WD 3.24	Position pointer over row's bottom border, press and hold down ALT and mouse button, drag to adjust row height to desired measurement as indicated in vertical ruler
Table row, add or delete border	WD 3.28	Select line weight and style on Table and Borders toolbar, click [icon], click [icon] on cell borders; to delete, select No Border as line style
Table row, delete	WD 3.21	Select row, click Table, point to Delete, click Rows
Table row, insert at end of table	WD 3.21	Position insertion point in lower-right cell at end of table, press Tab
Table row, insert within table	WD 3.21	Select row below, then click [icon] or click Table, point to Insert, and click Rows Above
Table text, rotate	WD 3.31	Select cells, click [icon] on the Tables and Borders toolbar
Table, center on page	WD 3.32	Click in table, click Table, click Table Properties, click Table tab, click Center Alignment option, click OK
Table, create	WD 3.13	Click [icon], drag pointer to select desired number of columns and rows; or click [icon] on Tables and Borders toolbar, draw desired number of columns and rows
Table, shade	WD 3.29	Select table area, click [icon] on Tables and Borders toolbar, and click a shading option

TASK	PAGE #	RECOMMENDED METHOD
Table, sort	WD 3.19	Click within column you want to sort by, click ⬇ or ⬇ on Tables and Borders toolbar
Tables and Borders toolbar, display	WD 3.20	Click ⊞
Text, align	WD 2.22	Select text, click ☰, ☰, ☰, or ☰
Text, copy by copy and paste	WD 2.13	Select text, click ⧉, move pointer to target location; then either click ⧉ or, if Clipboard opens, click item to paste in Clipboard
Text, copy by drag and drop	WD 2.12	Select text, press and hold down Ctrl and drag pointer to target location, release mouse button and Ctrl key
Text, delete	WD 2.09	Press Backspace key to delete character to left of insertion point; press the Delete key to delete character to right; press Ctrl + Backspace to delete to beginning of word; press Ctrl + Delete to delete to end of word
Text, find	WD 2.15	Click ⊙, click 🔍, type search text, click Find Next
Text, find and replace	WD 2.15	Click ⊙, click 🔍, click Replace tab, type search text, press Tab, type replacement text, click Find Next
Text, format	WD 2.29	See "Font Style, change"
Text, move by cut and paste	WD 2.13	Select text, click ✂, move to target location, click ⧉
Text, move by drag and drop	WD 2.12	Select text, drag pointer to target location, release mouse button
Text, select a block of	WD 2.09	Click at beginning of block, press and hold down Shift and click at end of block
Text, select a paragraph of	WD 2.09	Double-click in selection bar next to paragraph
Text, select a sentence of	WD 2.09	Press Ctrl and click within sentence
Text, select entire document of	WD 2.09	Press Ctrl and click in selection bar
Text, select multiple lines of	WD 2.09	Click and drag in selection bar
Text, select multiple paragraphs of	WD 2.09	Double-click and drag in selection bar
Toolbar, display	WD 1.08	Right-click any visible toolbar, click name of desired toolbar
Word, start	WD 1.05	Click Start, point to Programs, click Microsoft Word
Word, exit	WD 1.30	Close all open documents, then click ☒ on the title bar
WordArt object, create	WD 4.04	Click ◀, click desired WordArt style, type WordArt text, select font, size, and style, click OK

File Finder

Location in Tutorial	Name and Location of Data File	Student Saves File As...	Student Creates New File
WORD LEVEL 1, DISK 1			
Tutorial 1			
Session 1.2			Tutorial.01\Tutorial\Tacoma Job Fair Letter.doc
Review Assignments			Tutorial.01\Review\Job Fair Reminder.doc
Case Problem 1			Tutorial.01\Cases\Confirmation Letter.doc
Case Problem 2			Tutorial.01\Cases\Rock Climbing Request Letter.doc
Case Problem 3			Tutorial.01\Cases\Awards Memo.doc
Case Problem 4			Tutorial.01\Cases\My Template Letter.doc
Tutorial 2			
Session 2.1	Tutorial.02\Tutorial\Annuity.doc	Tutorial.02\Tutorial\RHS Annuity Plan.doc	
Session 2.2	Tutorial.02\Tutorial\RHS\Annuity Plan.doc (*Saved from Session 2.1*)	Tutorial.02\Tutorial\RHS Annuity Plan Copy 2.doc Tutorial.02\Tutorial\RHS Annuity Plan Final Copy.doc	
Review Assignments	Tutorial.02\Review\RHSQuart.doc Tutorial.02\Review\RHSPort.doc	Tutorial.02\Review\RHSQuarterly Report.doc Tutorial.02\Review\RHS Portfolio Changes	
Case Problem 1	Tutorial.02\Cases\Store.doc	Tutorial.02\Cases\Store-It-All Policies.doc	
Case Problem 2	Tutorial.02\Cases\UpTime.doc	Tutorial.02\Cases\UpTime Training Summary.doc	
Case Problem 3	Tutorial.02\Cases\Ridge	Tutorial.02\Cases\Ridge Top Guide.doc	
Case Problem 4			Tutorial.02\Cases\Restaurant Review.doc Tutorial.02\Cases\Edited Restaurant Review.doc
Tutorial 3			
Session 3.1	Tutorial.03\Tutorial\EverRipe.doc	Tutorial.03\Tutorial\EverRipe Report.doc Tutorial.03\Tutorial\EverRipe Report Copy 2.doc	
Session 3.2	Tutorial.03\Tutorial\EverRipe Report Copy 2.doc (*Saved from Session 3.1*)	Tutorial.03\Tutorial\EverRipe Report Final Copy.doc	
Review Assignments	Tutorial.03\Review\StatRep.doc Tutorial.03\Review\ZonReq.doc Tutorial.03\Review\Members.doc	Tutorial.03\Review\AgTech Status Report.doc Tutorial.03\Review\Zoning Request.doc Tutorial.03\Review\Zoning Board Members.doc	
Case Problem 1	Tutorial.03\Cases\OceanRep.doc	Tutorial.03\Cases\Ocean Breeze Report.doc	
Case Problem 2	Tutorial.03\Cases\Europe.doc	Tutorial.03\Cases\Europe Tour Report.doc	
Case Problem 3	Tutorial.03\Cases\Classics.doc	Tutorial.03\Cases\Classical Music CDs.doc	
Case Problem 4			Tutorial.03\Cases\Bright Star Training.doc
Tutorial 4			
Session 4.1	Tutorial.04\Tutorial\MiniInfo.doc	Tutorial.04\Tutorial\FastFad Newsletter.doc	
Session 4.2	Tutorial.04\Tutorial\FastFad Newsletter.doc (*Saved from Session 4.1*)	Tutorial.04\Tutorial\FastFad Newsletter Final Copy.doc	
Review Assignments	Tutorial.04\Review\FigSpecs.doc	Tutorial.04\Review\Action Pros.doc	
Case Problem 1	Tutorial.04\Cases\CityComp.doc Tutorial.04\Cases\Knight.bmp	Tutorial.04\Cases\Computer.doc	
Case Problem 2	Tutorial.04\Cases\MSM_NEWS.doc	Tutorial.04\Cases\MSM Newsletter.doc	
Case Problem 3	Tutorial.04\Cases\Wellness.doc	Tutorial.04\Cases\Wellness Newsletter.doc	
Case Problem 4			Tutorial.04\Cases\New Home.doc